SUCCESS IN THE NEW RETIREMENT

Steps to Successfully Navigate the New Retirement

F3E

Foundation for Financial Education

Table of Contents

1. The Foundation of the New Retirement

2. Keys to Success in the New Retirement

Section 1

The Foundation of the New Retirement

Retirement is Changing

The old metaphor for retirement was the three-legged stool:

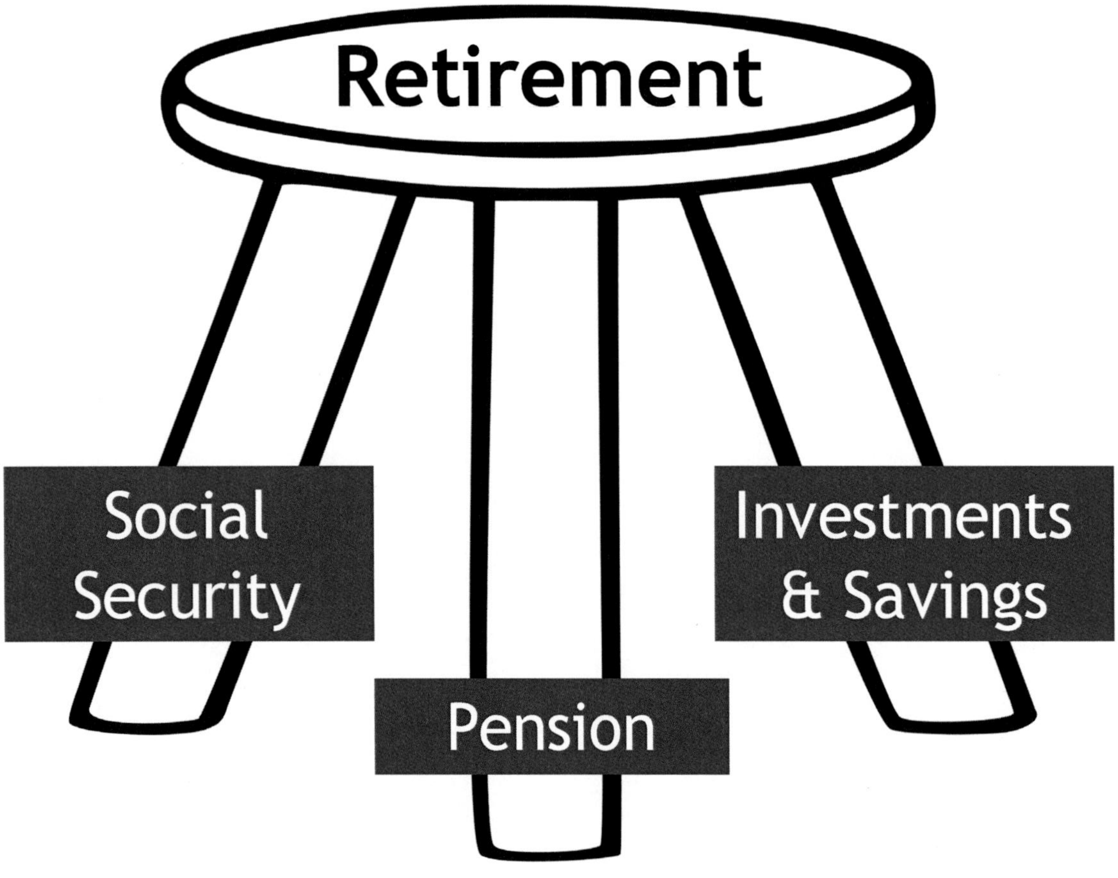

Retirement is Changing

We Are Living Longer

If you're 65 today, the probability of living to a specific age or beyond

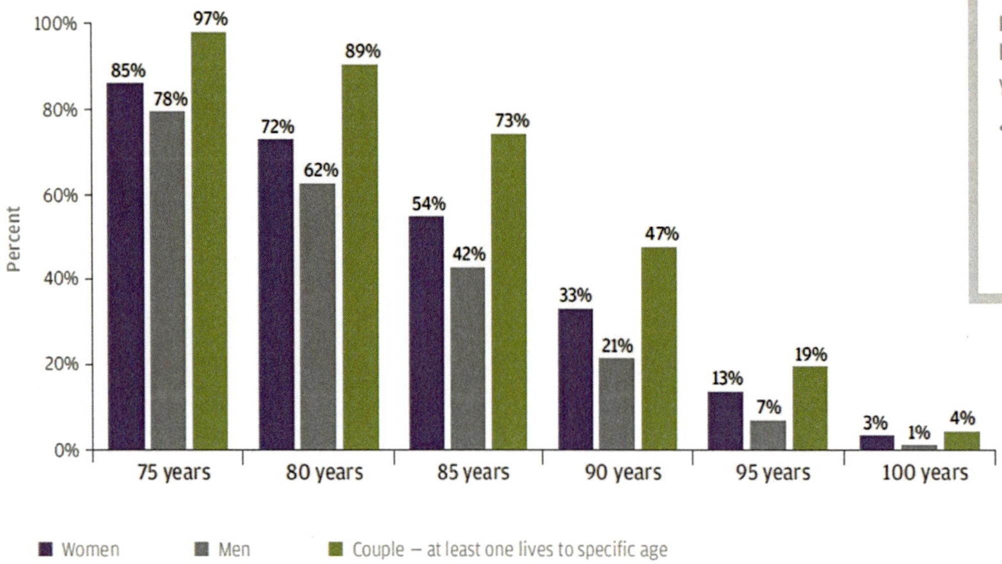

COUNT ON LONGEVITY

Life expectancy tells only half the story. Plan on the probability of living much longer, perhaps 30 plus years in retirement.

- For example, there is a 47% chance that one spouse will live to age 90 or beyond.

The Keys to Building A Successful Retirement

- Recognize and accept that the rules of the game have changed.
- Realize that retirement today is not hopeless or impossible; it's just different.
- Take appropriate steps:

EDUCATION

ACTION

ADJUSTMENT AND MODIFICATION

Social Security and the New Retirement

Section Objectives:

- What are the financial issues facing Social Security?
- What are the causes of these issues?
- What are the solutions and how can they impact you?

Note: The following information contained is provided for general educational purposes only. This information and the presenter are not affiliated with the Social Security Administration or any other government agency.

Social Security: Who's Supporting the System?

What Social Security Means To You

This *Social Security Statement* can help you plan for your financial future. It provides estimates of your Social Security benefits under current law and updates your latest reported earnings.

Please read this *Statement* carefully. If you see a mistake, please let us know. That's important because your benefits will be based on our record of your lifetime earnings. We recommend you keep a copy of your *Statement* with your financial records.

Social Security is for people of all ages...
We're more than a retirement program. Social Security also can provide benefits if you become disabled and help support your family after you die.

Work to build a secure future...
Social Security is the largest source of income for most elderly Americans today, but Social Security was never intended to be your only source of income when you retire. You also will need other savings, investments, pensions or retirement accounts to make sure you have enough money to live comfortably when you retire.

security for its workers and their families. Now, however, the Social Security system is facing serious financial problems, and action is needed soon to make sure the system will be sound when today's younger workers are ready for retirement.

Without changes, in 2033 the Social Security Trust Fund will be able to pay only about 77 cents for each dollar of scheduled benefits.* We need to resolve these issues soon to make sure Social Security continues to provide a foundation of protection for future generations.

Social Security on the Net...
Visit *www.socialsecurity.gov* on the Internet to learn more about Social Security. You can read publications, including *When To Start Receiving Retirement Benefits*; use our Retirement Estimator to obtain immediate and personalized estimates of future benefits; and when you're ready to apply for benefits, use our improved online application—It's so easy!

Without changes, in 2033 the Social Security Trust Fund will be able to pay only about 77 cents for each dollar of scheduled benefits.* We need to resolve these issues soon to make sure Social Security continues to provide a foundation of protection for future generations.

Social Security:
Who's Supporting the System?

1940: For every recipient of Social Security, there were 159 taxpaying workers paying into the system. (Social Security Answer Book, pg. I-5)

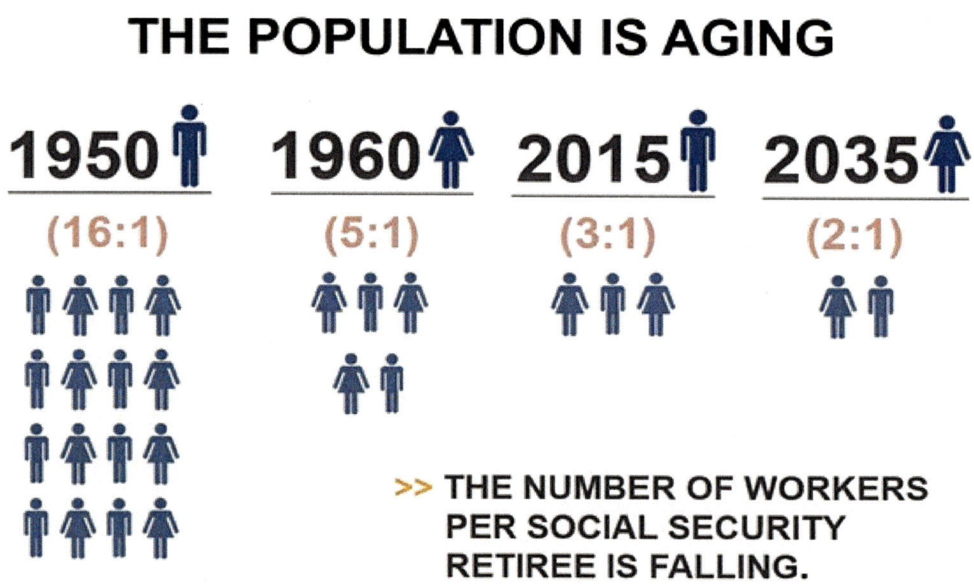

Source: 2015 Social Security Trustees Report

Increasing Life Expectancy

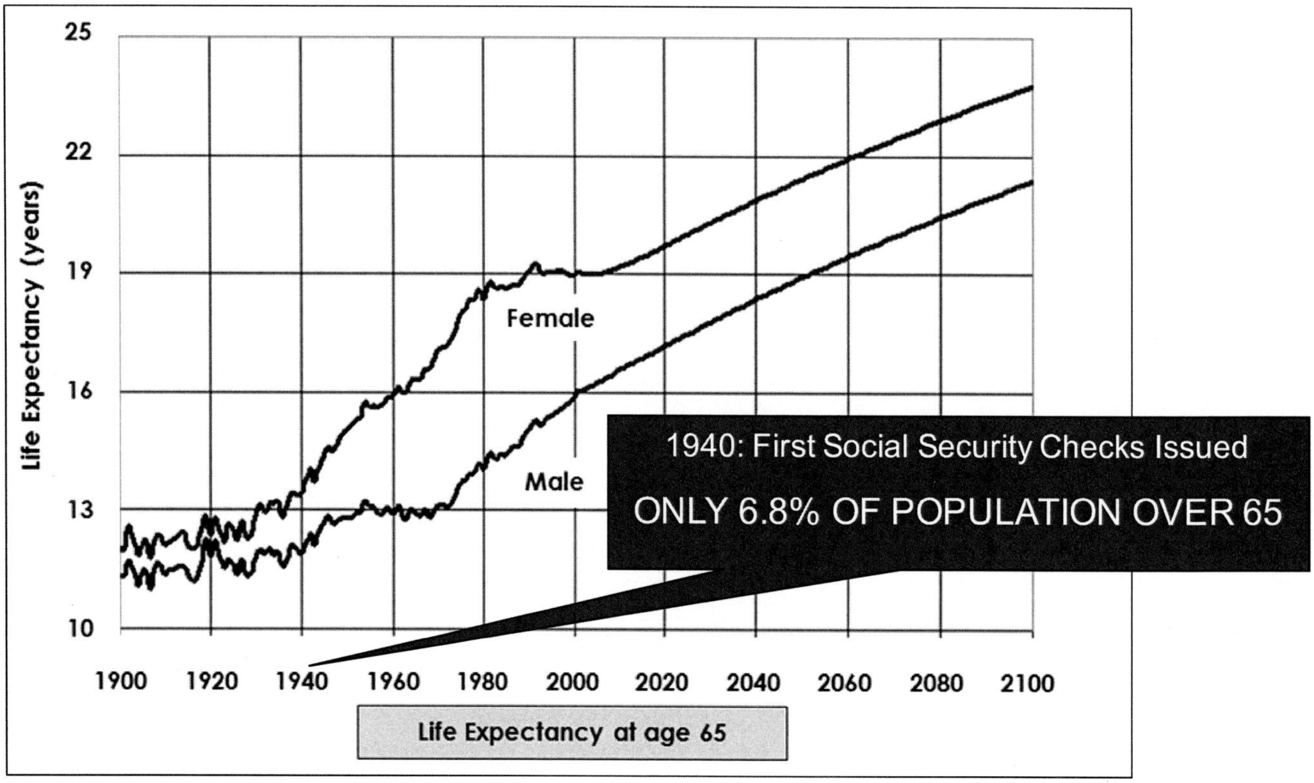

Source: Social Security Administration, Office of the Chief Actuary. Life Tables for the United States Social Security Area 1900–2100, August 2005, SSA Pub. No. 11-11536.

This Is Not a New Problem

- LESSONS FROM 1983:

  - Payroll taxes gradually increased from 8.05% to 12.4%.
  - Full retirement age increased from 65 to 67.
  - SS increase for delaying benefits raised from 3% to 8%.
  - Social Security benefits included as taxable income.

- RECENT CHANGES:

  "File and Suspend" and "Restricted Spousal" strategies eliminated or restricted.

Source: https://www.ssa.gov/history/1983amend.html

WORKING INCOME AFTER CLAIMING SS

Impact of Possible Changes

- INCREASE THE PAYROLL TAX (12.4%)

Option 1:

Increase it to 15.2% from 2028 to 2057 and 18% from 2058 and beyond.

- **ESTIMATED RESULT:** Eliminates 100% of funding shortfall and creates a surplus.

Option 2:

Gradually increase it by 0.1% per year for 20 years, until it reached 14.4%.

- **ESTIMATED RESULT:** Eliminates 49% of the shortfall.

Note: These are hypothetical examples and scenarios.

Impact of Possible Changes

- RAISE THE RETIREMENT AGE

Option 1:

Raise Full Retirement Age to age 70 by two months per year for anyone born after 1960.

- **ESTIMATED RESULT:** Eliminates 50% of the shortfall.

Option 2:

Raise the age of early retirement from age 62 to 64.

- **ESTIMATED RESULT:** Eliminates 30% of the shortfall.

Note: These are hypothetical examples and scenarios.

Impact of Possible Changes

- Cost of Living Adjustments (COLA)
  - 2015 COLA = 1.7%
  - 2016 COLA = 0.0%
  - 2017 COLA = 0.3%
  - 2018 COLA = 2.0%
- REDUCE COST OF LIVING ADJUSTMENTS (COLAs)

Option: Inflation adjustments based on the Chained CPI

Chained CPI - Assumes that consumers change their purchasing habits when prices increase

- **ESTIMATED RESULT:** Eliminates 19% of the shortfall.

Note: These are hypothetical examples and scenarios.

Pensions and the New Retirement

Section Objectives:

- What is changing in regard to pensions?
- What are the potential issues facing many pension plans today?
- What protections are in place for pensions?
- What is replacing pensions?

Disappearing Pensions

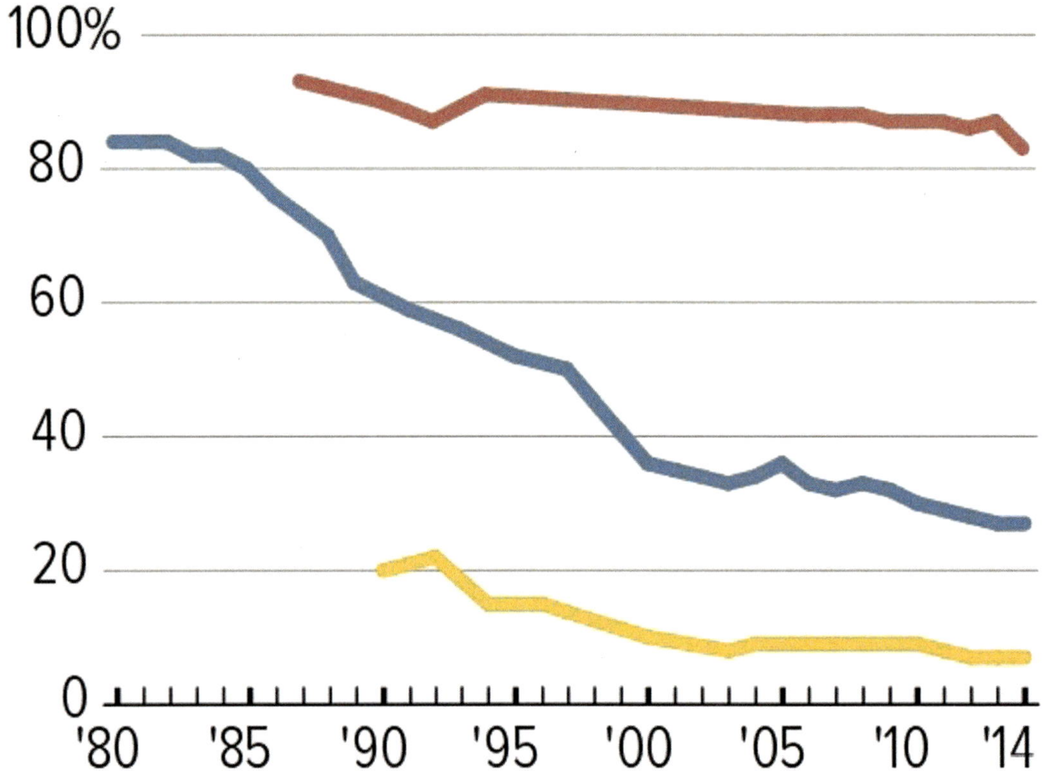

Percentage of full-time workers covered by defined-benefit pension plans

- State and local government
- Medium and large private establishments
- Small private establishments

Source: Employee Benefir Research Institute, EBRI Databook on Employee Benefits, Chapter 10 (www.ebri.org); Bureau of Labor Statistics.

Why Are Many Pensions Disappearing?

FAILED ASSUMPTIONS:

- Life Expectancy

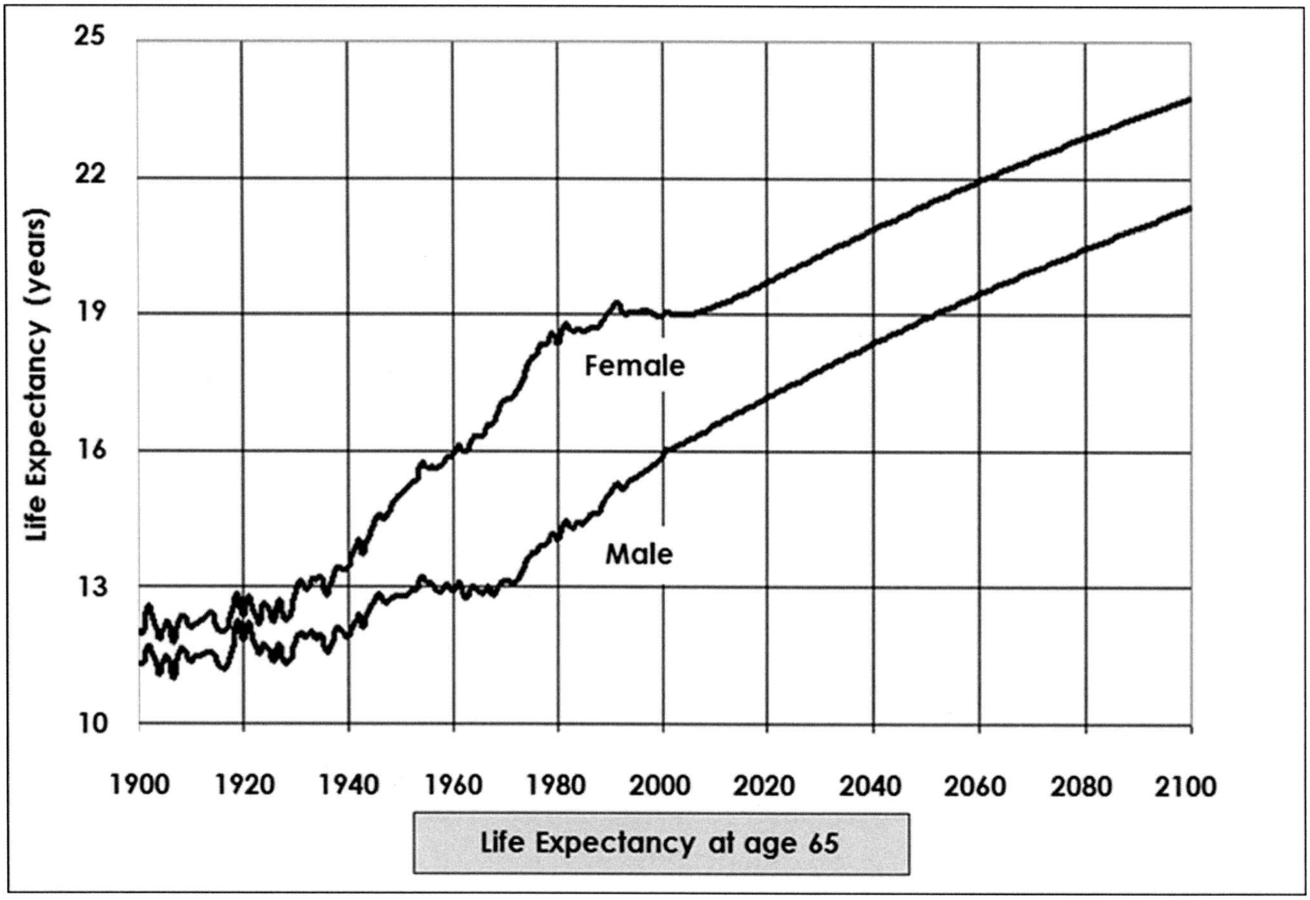

Source: Social Security Administration, Office of the Chief Actuary. Life Tables for the United States Social Security Area 1900–2100, August 2005, SSA Pub. No. 11-11536.

Why Are Many Pensions Disappearing?

FAILED ASSUMPTIONS:

- Rate of Return

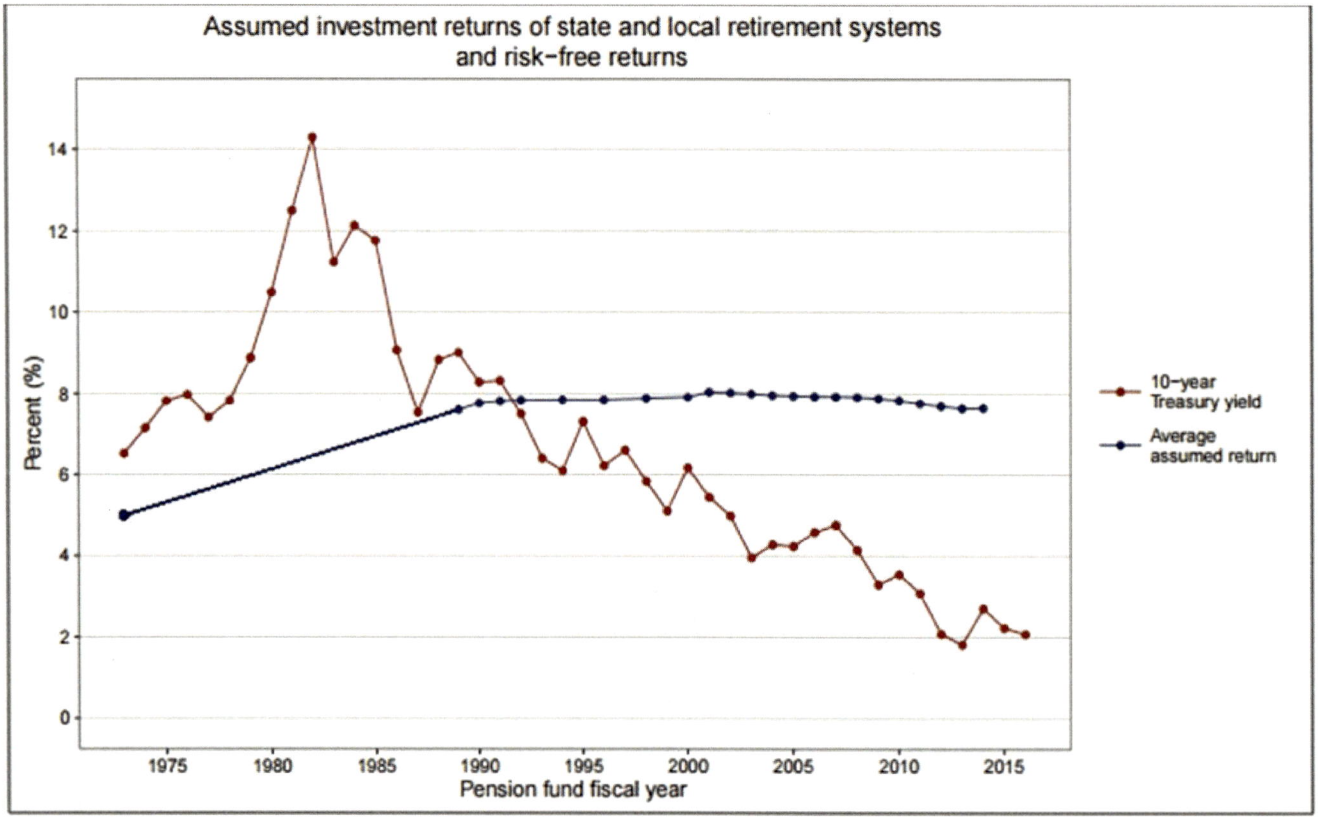

Source: The Rockefeller Institute of Government.

Many Pensions Are Becoming Underfunded

- Pension Benefit Guaranty Corporation (PBGC) offers protection to some pension plans.
- Upon termination of participating plans, PBGC's program pays the benefit provided up to the limits set by law. To find out if your plan is a participant, go to PBGC.gov.
- Corporations pay a premium to insure their pension plans.
    - Premium costs are expected to rise 25% over the next four years to try and address the shortfall.

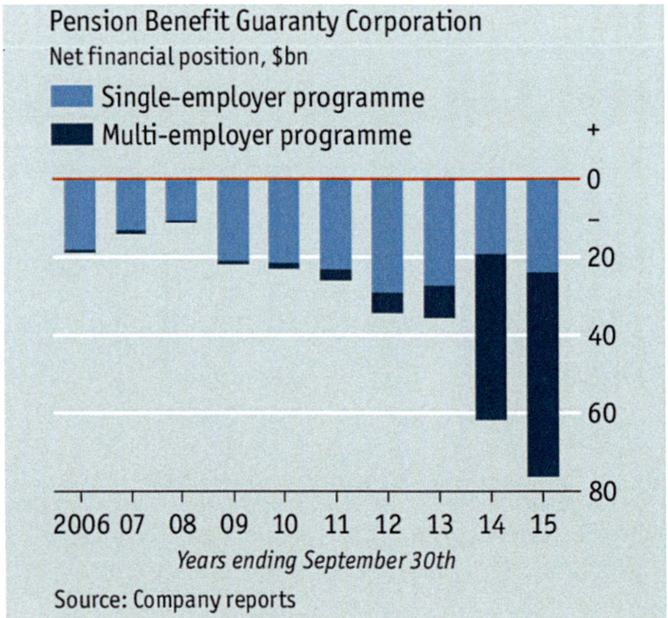

Source: http://www.economist.com/news/finance-and-economics/21696540-americas-congress-has-allowed-pension-insurance-scheme-become-dangerously

What Is Replacing Pensions?

What Do They All Have in Common?

Estate Planning in the New Retirement

Section Objectives:

- What is probate and how can you avoid it?
- What documents are needed for a properly designed estate plan?

Note: The following information contained is provided for general educational purposes only and is not intended as legal or tax advice on any subject matter.

The Probate Process

pro·bate	Noun	1. The official proving of a will.
'prō,bāt/	Verb	1. Establish the validity of (a will).

Time Delay

Usually takes 4–12 months. Often determined by the time mandated by the state to notify creditors.

Cost

The fee can be a flat fee or a % of the value of the estate.

(Fees vary by state)

Public Process

Matter of public record, false claims on estate

Source: http://www.nolo.com/legal-encyclopedia/five-myths-about-wills-probate.html

Avoiding Probate

- Proper beneficiary designations

Beneficiary on Accounts

Specific beneficiary designations on individual accounts

Beneficiary Deed

Used to designate beneficiaries on real estate (available in some states)

Revocable Living Trust

Designates a trustee that can administer estate after the death of the grantor

Tips for Using a Revocable Living Trust

- Special family circumstances (e.g., second marriage)
- One or more beneficiary is disabled or cannot receive assets in their name
- Control how assets are distributed from the grave
- Own real estate in a state where beneficiary deeds are not allowed
- Simplify beneficiary designations

Other Legal Documents

Financial Power of Attorney (Durable Power of Attorney)	• Allows a designated beneficiary to handle financial affairs if you become incapacitated (unable to make decisions for yourself)
Health Care Power of Attorney	• Grants another person decision-making authority should you become unable to make health care decisions on your own
Living Will (Health care directive)	• Allows you to state your wishes for end-of-life medical care

By having proper documents in place, you can help prevent your loved ones from being **forced to get court supervision** to make decisions on your behalf.

Long-Term Care (LTC) in the New Retirement

Section Objectives:

- What are the rules in regard to long-term care benefits?
- What are the options to plan and prepare for long-term care needs?

Long-Term Care & Longevity

With the average life expectancy surpassing age 85, the number of people who will require some sort of assistance performing daily living functions can be expected to increase dramatically.

As a Result of Physical and Cognitive Impairments, 70% of Seniors Will Need Long-Term Service and Support

7 IN 10
AMERICANS AGED 65 YEARS OR OLDER

THE AVERAGE LENGTH OF TIME A SENIOR ADULT WILL NEED ASSISTANCE WITH ACTIVITIES OF DAILY LIVING IS 3 YEARS

Source: www.longtermcare.gov

Paying for Long-Term Care

Personal Resources:

- Self-insured (spend own assets)
- Family and Friends
- Long-term care insurance

Government Resources:

- Medicaid

Medicaid Spend-Down Guidelines: You must meet certain asset qualifications before you qualify for Medicaid

Single Person	No more than $2,000 in assets
Married Person	Countable assets are limited to: • $120,900 of liquid assets • Primary residence • One car

Medicaid also limits the amount of income a spouse can receive:

Monthly maintenance needs allowance: $2,003 – $3,023

Note: Figures vary by state.
Source: https://www.azahcccs.gov

Long-Term Care Insurance

Traditional LTC Insurance

- Underwriting based on morbidity not mortality
- Premiums can increase or benefits can be reduced
- Expenses paid through reimbursement
- No benefit if not used for long-term care

Life Insurance w/ LTC Rider

- Underwriting based on mortality
- Premiums cannot increase
- Benefits paid if requirements met
- Benefit is paid out as an accelerated benefit or as a death benefit

Your Money in the New Retirement

Section Objectives:

- How do emotions impact our investment decisions?
- Common security investments
- What are the different types of annuities and how do they differ?
- Understanding the value proposition

Emotions & Investing

Emotional Smoothing

- Hindsight returns vs. Real-time volatility
- Emotions impact our ability to make decisions

Benefits of reduced volatility

- Remain committed to investment strategy

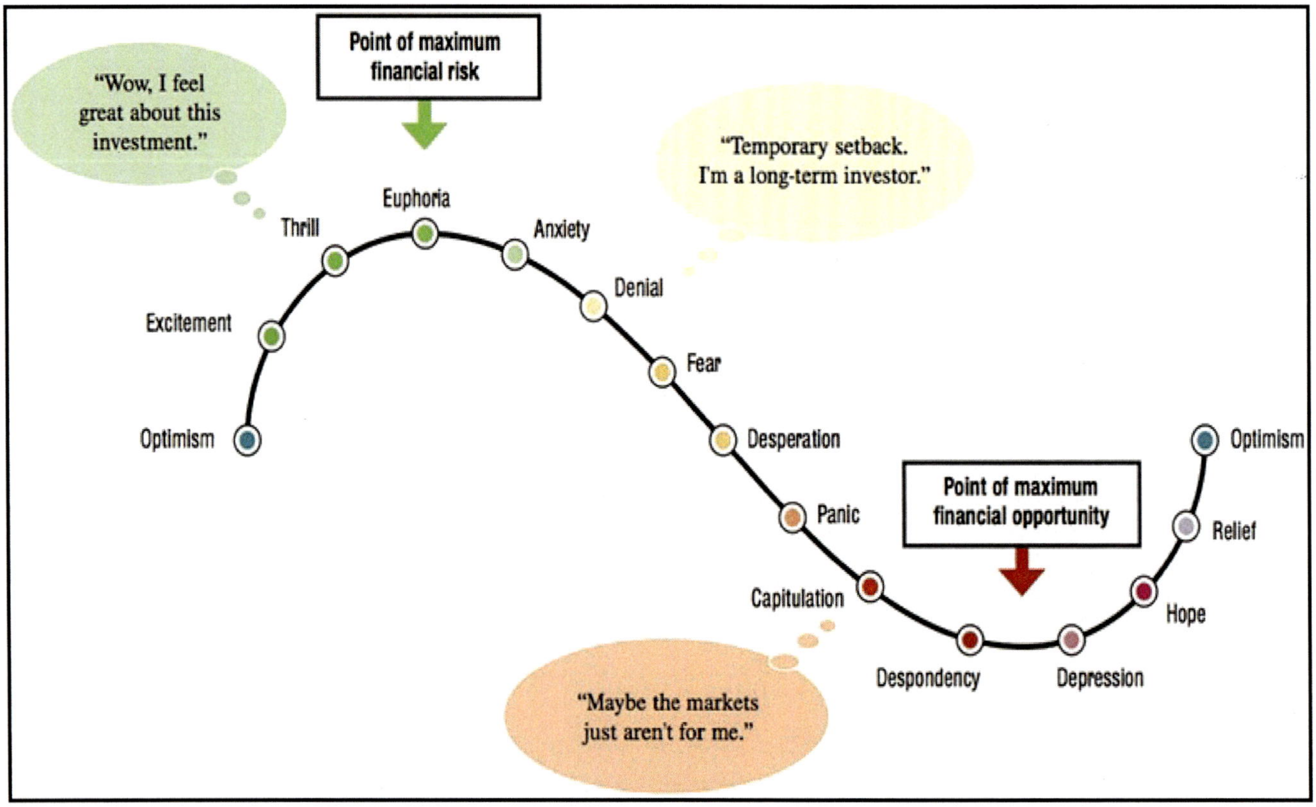

Chart Source: Westcore Funds / Denver Investment Advisors, LLC, 1998

Investments/Securities

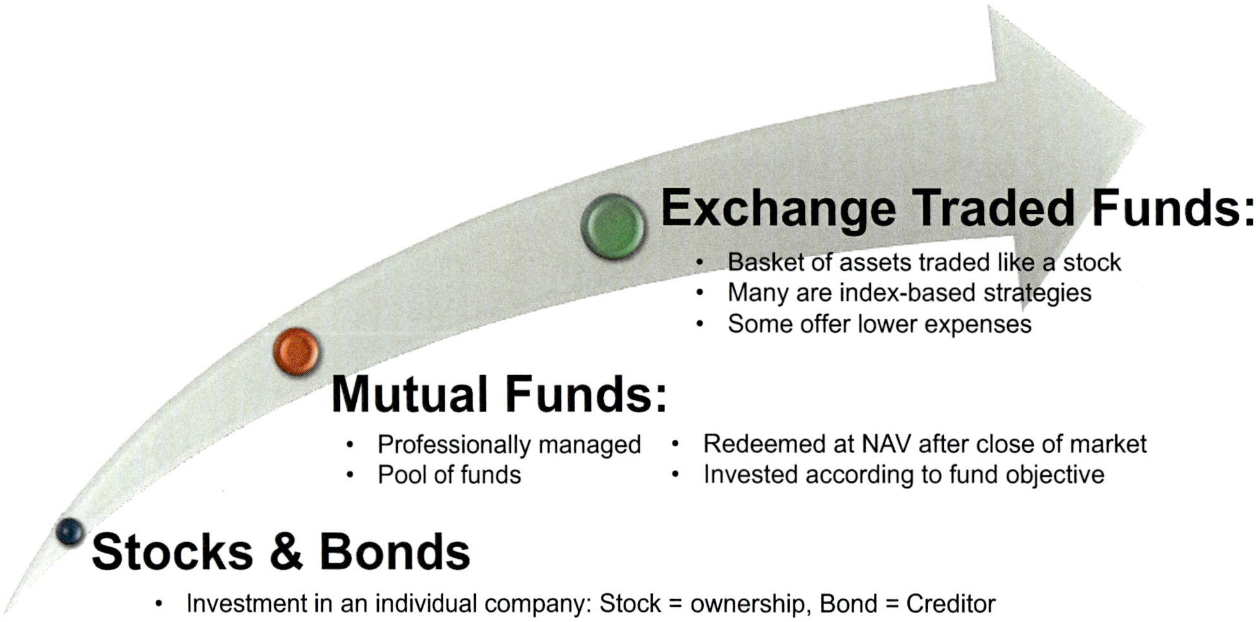

The Inherent Problem with MFs & ETFs

"Any mutual fund or ETF with a name suggesting that it focuses on a particular type of investment must invest at least 80% of its assets in the type of investment suggested by its name."

Source: SEC, Mutual Funds and ETFS, A Guide for Investors

Less than 26% of mutual funds outperformed their benchmark.

Source: Morningstar Fund Analysis, 2015

Myths About Annuities

"Get your facts first, and then you can distort them as much as you please."

- Mark Twain

MYTH: All annuities are the same.

FACT: There are several different types of annuities. Each type has its pros and cons.

MYTH: Once you put money into an annuity, you will never have access to it again.

FACT: Most annuities offer a lump sum at the end of the contract or at death (whichever is earlier).

MYTH: Annuities should not be considered as part of a retirement plan.

FACT: Some annuities have been oversold but they can benefit a financial plan if used properly.

Common Annuity Types

	IMMEDIATE	FIXED	FIXED INDEXED	VARIABLE
RATE OF RETURN	Rate determines monthly payout	Guaranteed interest rate	Upside potential; return limited by crediting strategy	Return based on performance of chosen sub-accounts
PRINCIPAL PROTECTION	N/A	YES	YES	NO
TAX-DEFERRED GROWTH	Distributed interest is taxable.	YES	YES	YES
LIFETIME INCOME RIDER AVAILABLE	YES	YES	YES	YES
LUMP SUM AVAILABLE	NO	YES	YES	YES
WHO CAN BENEFIT	Someone seeking immediate monthly income	Someone seeking a fixed rate, often times higher than offered by a CD	Someone seeking more potential upside while still protecting principal	Someone willing to take market risk but wants tax deferral

Note: All contract and guarantees, including optional benefits, are backed exclusively by the strength and claims-paying ability of the issuing insurance company.

Variable Annuities

Pros:

- Tax-deferred growth
- Market investments
- Lifetime income rider available

Cons:

- Surrender charges (w/ free withdrawals)
- Higher fees
- No principal protection

Fixed Indexed Annuities

Pros:

- Tax-deferred growth
- Principal protection
- Index-linked gains
- Lifetime income rider available

Cons:

- Surrender charges (w/ free withdrawals)
- Lower potential growth

The Value Proposition

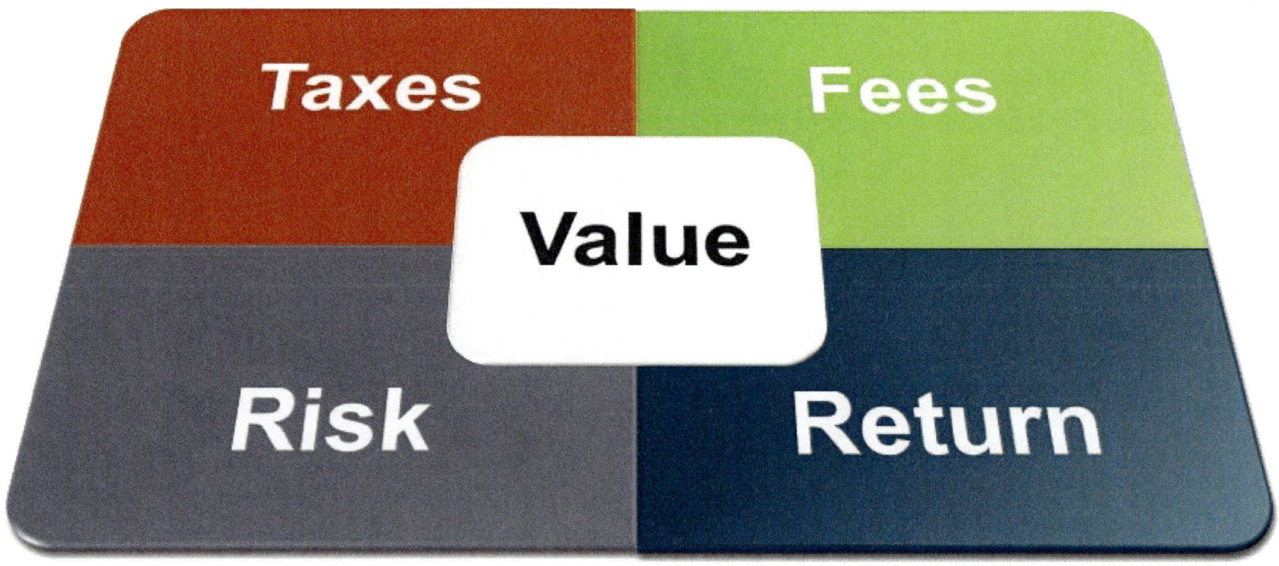

Section 2

Keys to Success in the New Retirement

Stage of Life Investing & Don't Lose It in the First Place

Section Objectives:

- Stage of Life Investing
- What are Target Date Funds?
- The "Two" Rules of 100
- Average vs. Actual Returns

Stage of Life Investing

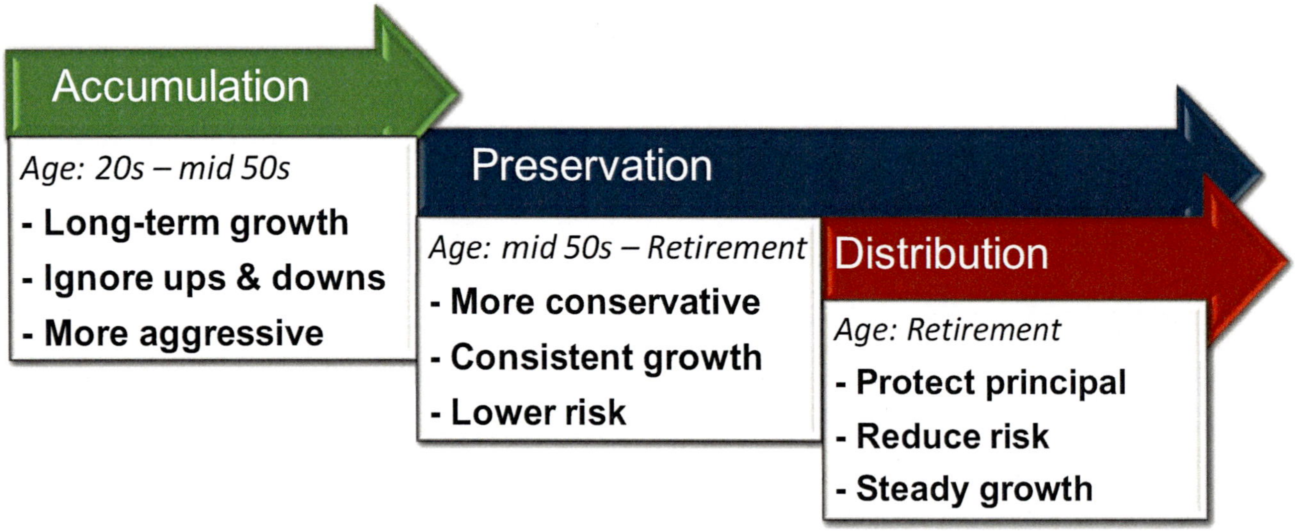

Stage of Life Investing

Years	Worst Dow Jones Return
35 Years	6.1%
20 Years	2.5%
10 Years	-1.9%
5 Years	-37.5%
1 Year	-52.7%

What is the standard withdrawal rate?

Will your money run out?

Source: http://observationsandnotes.blogspot.com

Target-Date Funds

- The rise of target-date funds can be traced back to the Pension Protection Act of 2006
- Designed to create a "glide path" that reduces risk as you approach retirement
- Attempts to put "Stage of Life Investing" on autopilot

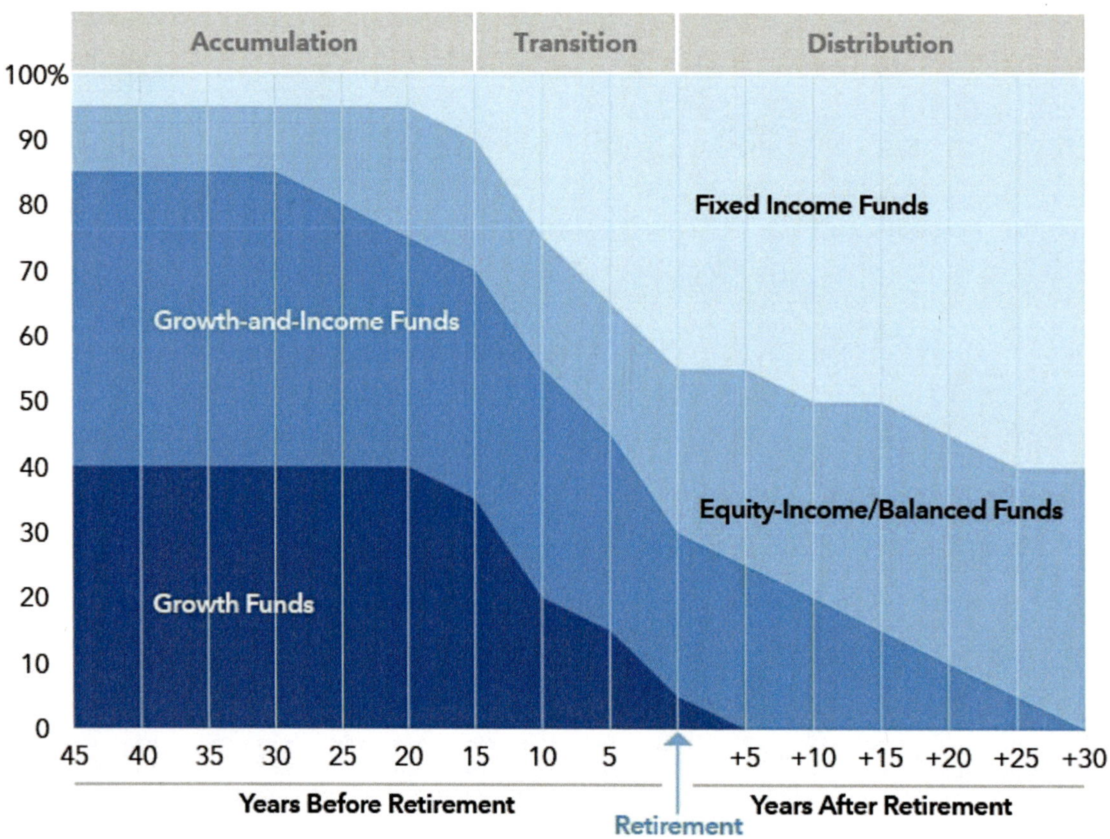

Target-Date Funds

MISCONCEPTIONS:

Target-Date Funds Survey:

- Only 30% correctly identified the meaning of the year in the fund's name
- 64% incorrectly believed the TDF would provide a guaranteed income stream in retirement

2010 Target-Date Fund Performance in 2008:

- Average loss was nearly: 24%
- Largest loss was: 41.22%
- Average fund still had more than 50% in stocks

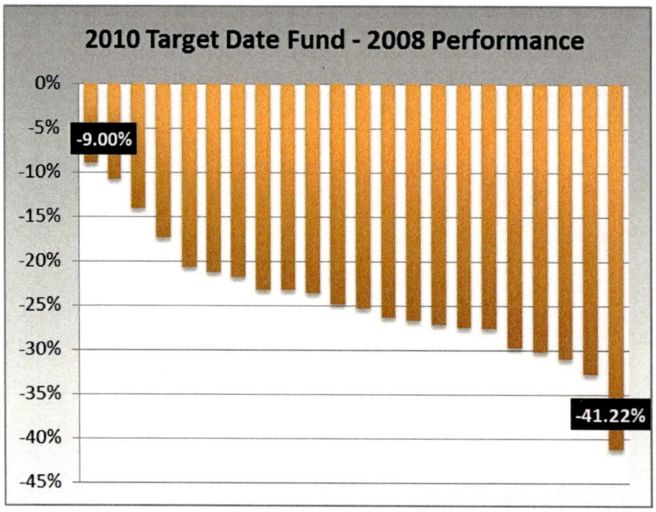

"Rule #1: Never lose money.
Rule #2: Never forget rule #1."
- Warren Buffett

The *Two* Rules of 100

Gains Needed to Offset Market Losses

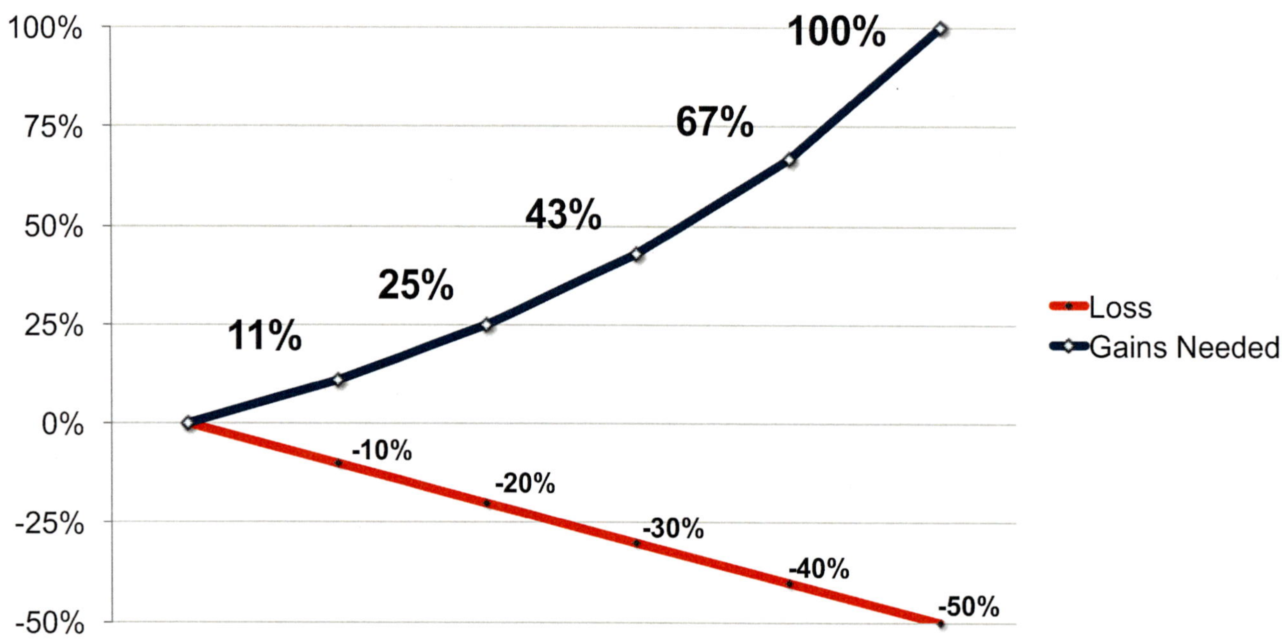

Average vs. Actual Returns

EXAMPLE:

- 8% Average Return

KEY TAKE AWAY:

- Actual return will always be lower than the average return when there are negative rates

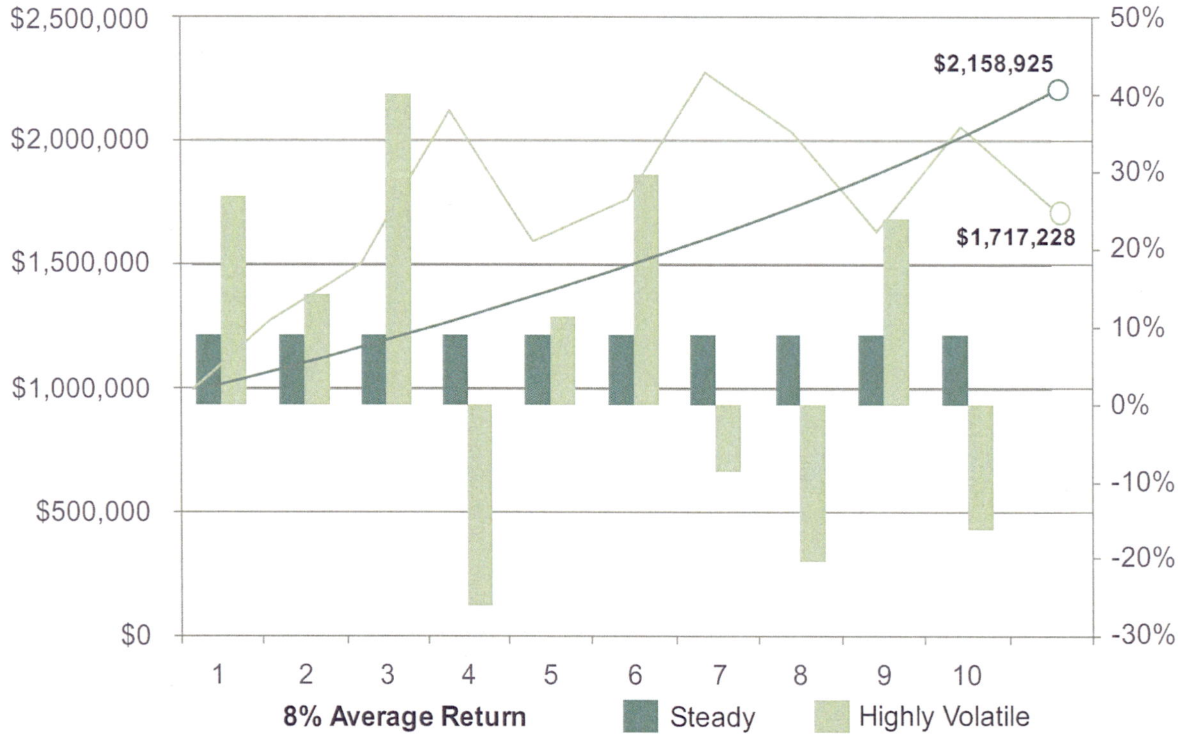

Note: The graph shown is hypothetical and does not represent any particular investment.

Correlation vs. Diversification

Section Objectives:

- What is correlation and how does it relate to diversification?
- Diversification is becoming more difficult?
- How to identify adjustments needed to diversify a portfolio?

Diversification

noun

the action of making or becoming more diverse or varied.

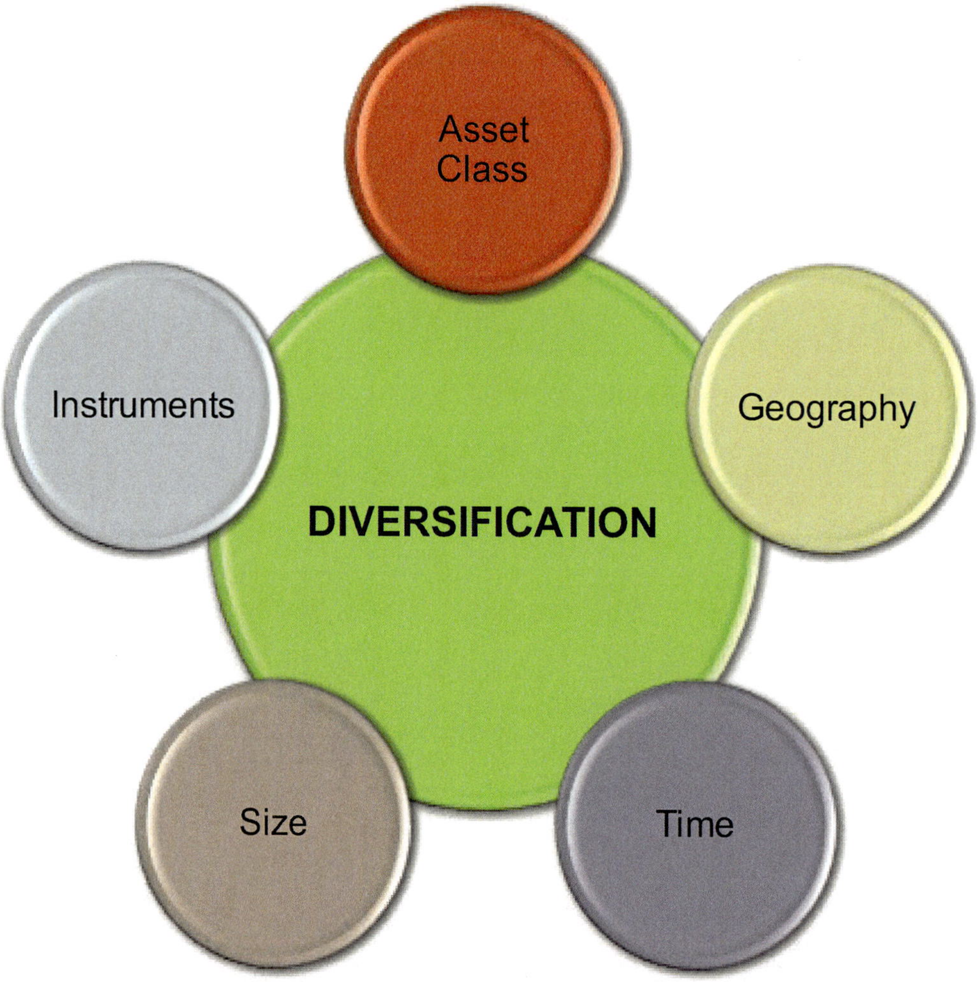

Correlation

Correlation determines how closely related the movements of one holding are to the various other holdings in a portfolio.

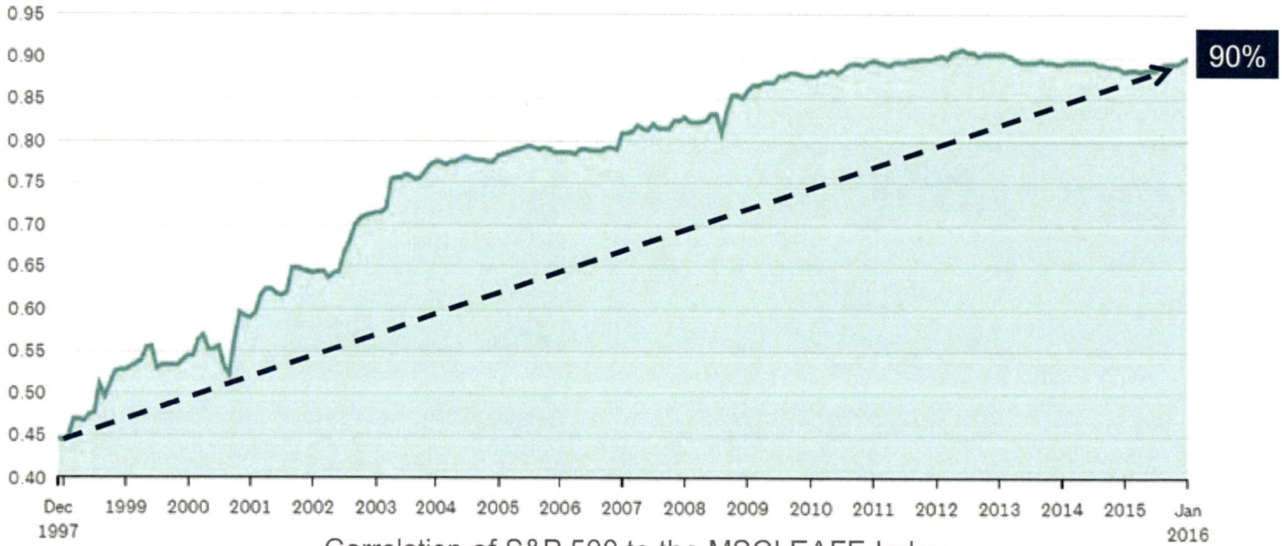

Correlation of S&P 500 to the MSCI EAFE Index

SOURCE: Bloomberg

Correlation Matrix

- Identify correlation between holdings
- Detect stock intersections
- Determine adjustments needed to achieve diversification

Correlation Matrix 3 Year

	1	2	3	4	5	6	7	8	9	10	11	12	13	14	15	16	17	18	19	20
1																				
2	-0.17																			
3	0.96	0.00																		
4	0.95	-0.18	0.92																	
5	0.79	0.05	0.92	0.75																
6	1.00	-0.16	0.96	0.94	0.79															
7	-0.03	0.97	0.16	-0.02	0.21	-0.02														
8	-0.14	0.99	0.04	-0.15	0.09	-0.13	0.98													
9	-0.29	0.93	-0.13	-0.31	-0.06	-0.28	0.87	0.94												
10	0.87	-0.31	0.81	0.94	0.62	0.86	-0.15	-0.27	-0.46											
11	0.82	0.02	0.93	0.77	0.98	0.82	0.17	0.05	-0.07	0.65										
12	0.55	0.47	0.72	0.54	0.79	0.54	0.62	0.50	0.32	0.40	0.75									
13	0.90	-0.22	0.85	0.95	0.66	0.90	-0.06	-0.20	-0.39	0.95	0.67	0.48								
14	0.92	-0.10	0.93	0.94	0.82	0.91	0.06	-0.07	-0.22	0.84	0.83	0.61	0.85							
15	0.78	0.19	0.90	0.72	0.96	0.78	0.32	0.21	0.07	0.58	0.95	0.78	0.63	0.79						
16	0.76	-0.10	0.86	0.73	0.93	0.75	0.05	-0.06	-0.17	0.62	0.96	0.66	0.62	0.78	0.88					
17	0.70	0.08	0.81	0.64	0.87	0.70	0.21	0.13	0.05	0.47	0.88	0.67	0.51	0.75	0.89	0.84				
18	0.15	0.01	0.21	0.11	0.28	0.15	0.05	0.02	0.02	0.12	0.26	0.16	0.07	0.23	0.24	0.30	0.26			
19	-0.24	0.91	-0.08	-0.29	0.00	-0.23	0.85	0.91	0.95	-0.47	-0.03	0.36	-0.37	-0.19	0.12	-0.12	0.08	-0.01		
20	0.12	0.90	0.29	0.13	0.30	0.13	0.95	0.89	0.73	0.02	0.26	0.68	0.11	0.18	0.40	0.14	0.24	0.07	0.73	

Investment Key

1 Vanguard Large Cap Index Institutional (USD, VLISX)
2 Vanguard Total Bond Market Index I (USD, VBTIX)
3 Vanguard Target Retirement 2030 Inv (USD, VTHRX)
4 Vanguard Mid Cap Index Institutional (USD, VMCIX)
5 Vanguard Total Intl Stock Index I (USD, VTSNX)
6 Vanguard S&P 500 ETF (USD, VOO)
7 Sterling Capital Total Return Bond I (USD, BIBTX)
8 Metropolitan West Total Return Bd I (USD, MWTIX)
9 DoubleLine Total Return Bond I (USD, DBLTX)
10 Vanguard Small Cap Index I (USD, VSCIX)
11 Vanguard FTSE Developed Markets ETF (USD, VEA)
12 Neuberger Berman Strategic Income I (USD, NSTLX)
13 Touchstone Mid Cap Value Inst (USD, TCVIX)
14 Goldman Sachs Growth Opportunities Instl (USD, GGOIX)
15 Harding Loevner International Eq Instl (USD, HLMIX)
16 Causeway International Value Instl (USD, CIVIX)
17 Morgan Stanley Inst Global Opp I (USD, MGGIX)
18 Fidelity® Government Cash Reserves (USD, FDRXX)
19 Vanguard Mortgage-Backed Secs ETF (USD, VMBS)
20 iShares US Credit Bond ETF (USD, CRED)

Degree of Correlation

High	Moderate	None	Moderately Negative	Highly Negative
0.70 to 1.00	0.11 to 0.69	0.10 to -0.10	-0.11 to -0.69	-0.70 to -1.00

Fees Really Do Matter

Section Objectives:

- Understanding the fees for each investment type
- The "real cost" of fees
- How to find out what you are paying

Fees of Common Investments

Fees and The Value Proposition

"Higher cost funds are more likely to underperform. Fees matter. They are one of the only reliable predictors of success."

"Funds with high costs, especially in bonds, tend to take greater risk."

- Morningstar Fee Study

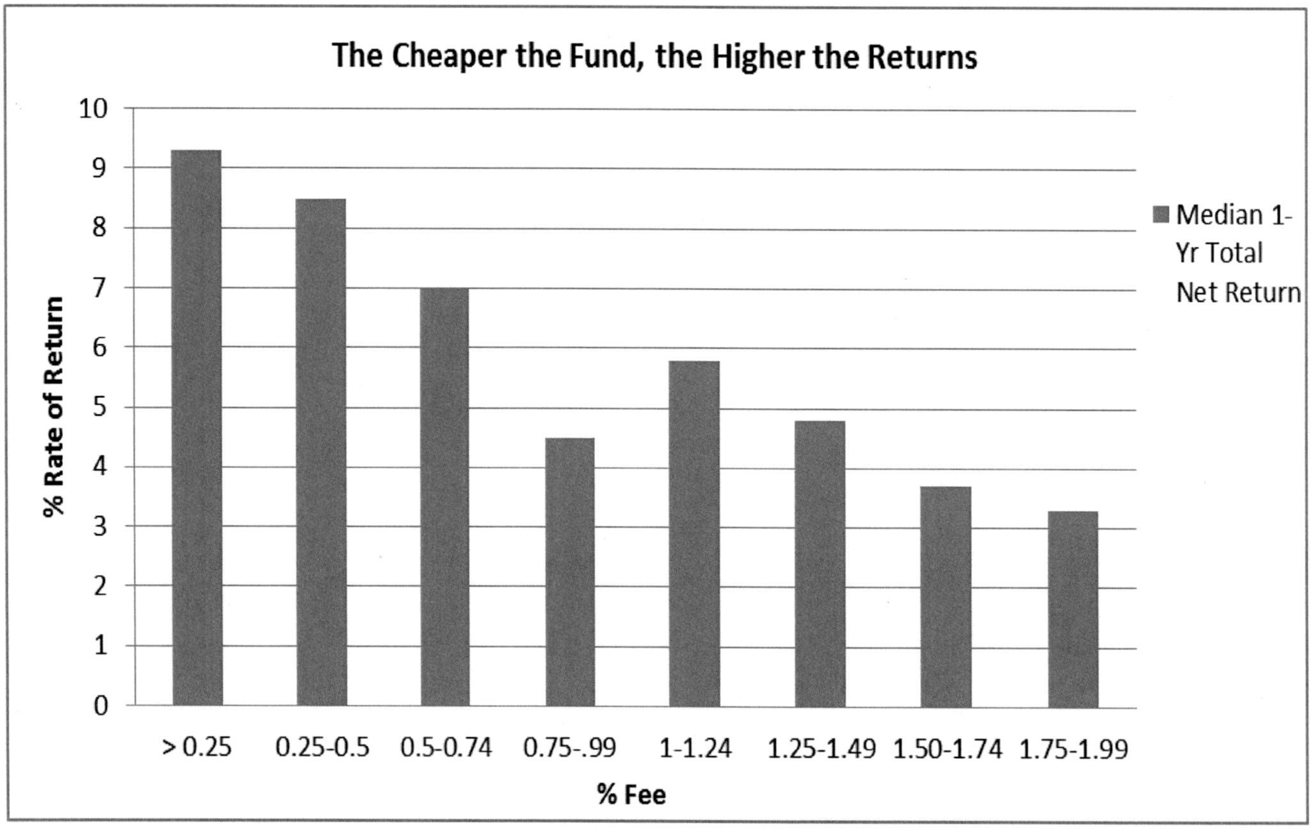

The Impact of Fees

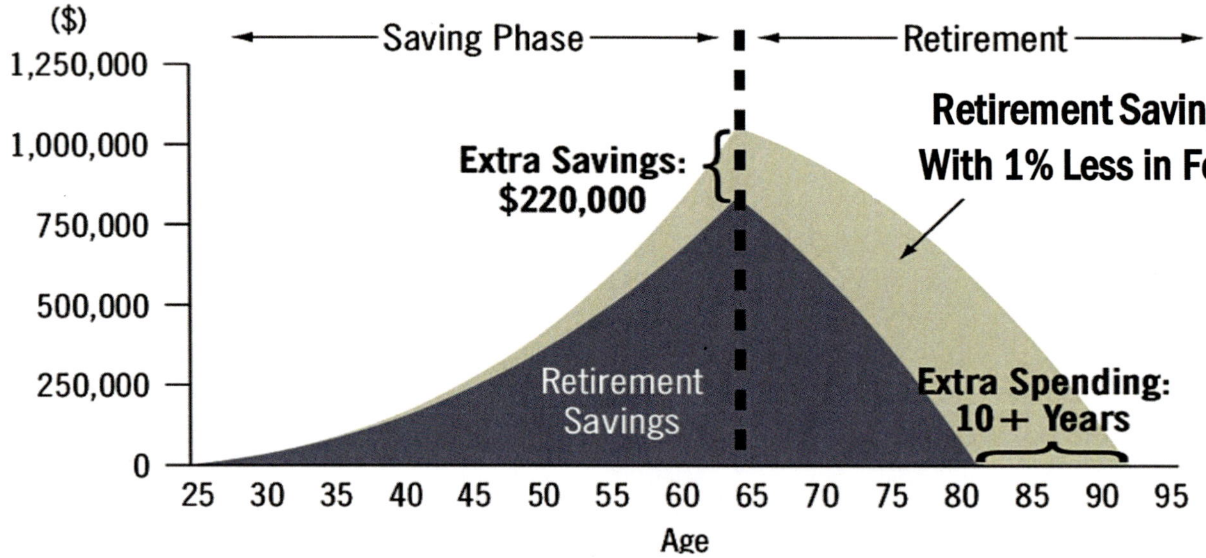

The saving phase simulates a salary of $45,000 increasing to $85,000, saving 8% per year increasing gradually to 15%. Retirement spending of $63,750 (75% of final salary). Rate of return of 9% assumed at age 25, linearly decreasing to 6% at age 80 and remaining constant thereafter. Source: AllianceBernstein

Analyze Your Accounts: Resources

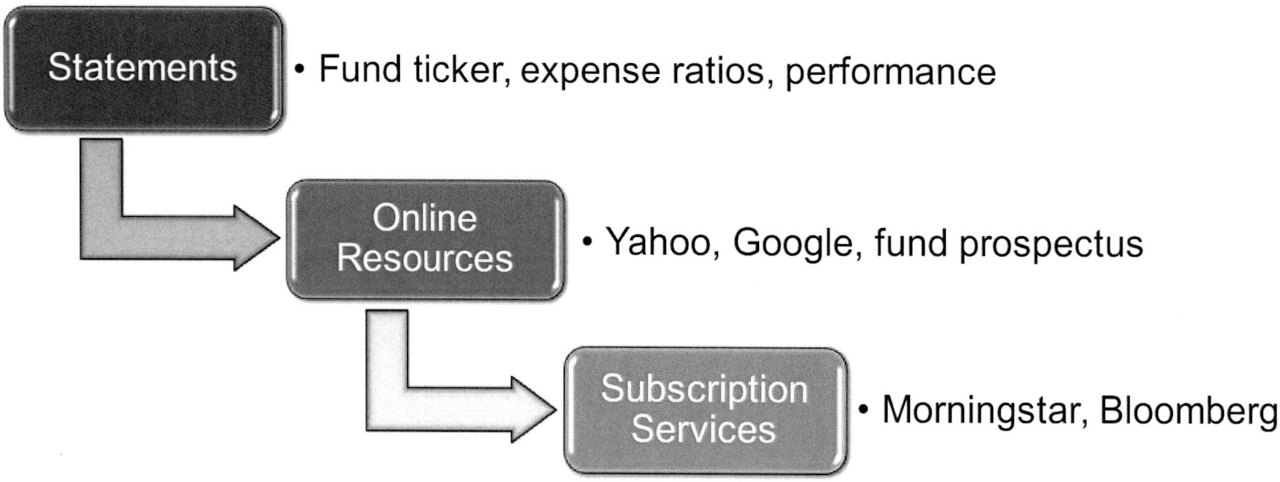

Tax Efficiency

Section Objectives:

- Assumptions regarding taxes during retirement
- Current and future taxes
- Steps you can take to be more tax efficient
- Roth conversion example

Assumptions Regarding Taxes

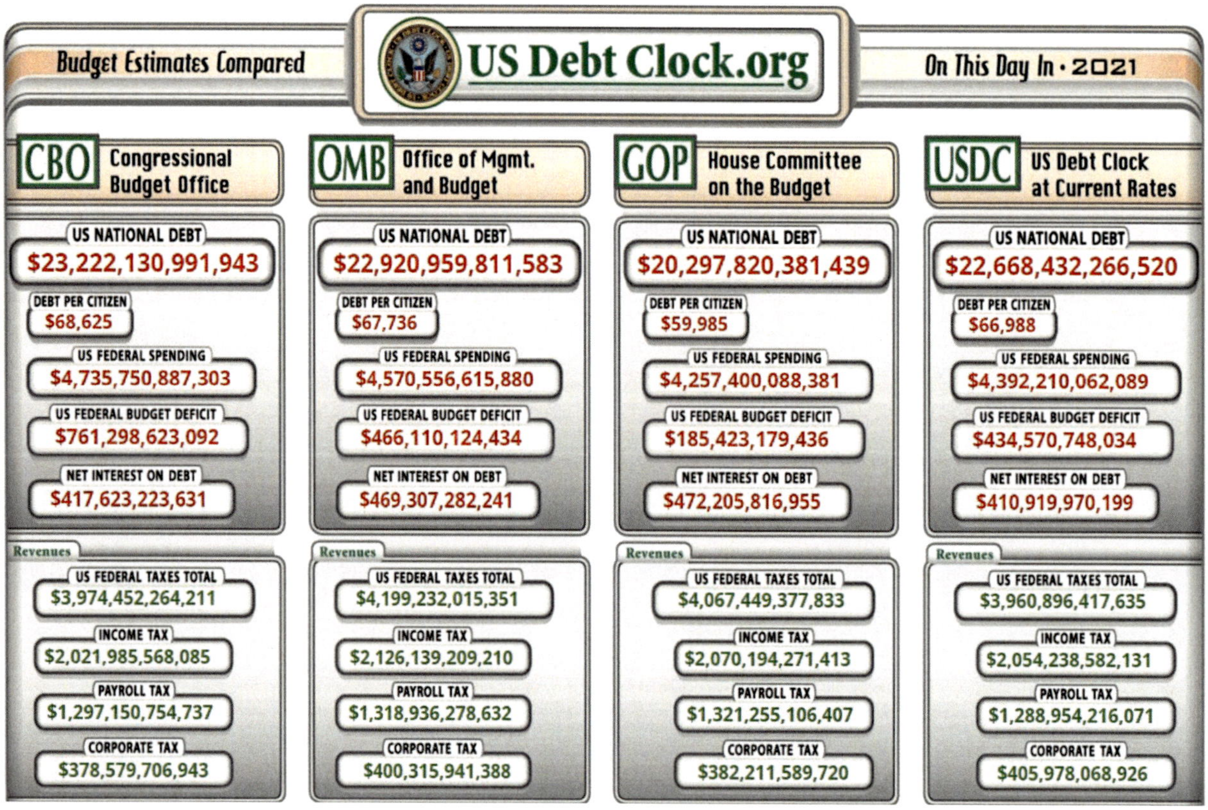
Budget Estimates Compared
US Debt Clock.org
On This Day In • 2021
CBO Congressional Budget Office
US NATIONAL DEBT $23,222,130,991,943
DEBT PER CITIZEN $68,625
US FEDERAL SPENDING $4,735,750,887,303
US FEDERAL BUDGET DEFICIT $761,298,623,092
NET INTEREST ON DEBT $417,623,223,631
Revenues
US FEDERAL TAXES TOTAL $3,974,452,264,211
INCOME TAX $2,021,985,568,085
PAYROLL TAX $1,297,150,754,737
CORPORATE TAX $378,579,706,943
OMB Office of Mgmt. and Budget
US NATIONAL DEBT $22,920,959,811,583
DEBT PER CITIZEN $67,736
US FEDERAL SPENDING $4,570,556,615,880
US FEDERAL BUDGET DEFICIT $466,110,124,434
NET INTEREST ON DEBT $469,307,282,241
Revenues
US FEDERAL TAXES TOTAL $4,199,232,015,351
INCOME TAX $2,126,139,209,210
PAYROLL TAX $1,318,936,278,632
CORPORATE TAX $400,315,941,388
GOP House Committee on the Budget
US NATIONAL DEBT $20,297,820,381,439
DEBT PER CITIZEN $59,985
US FEDERAL SPENDING $4,257,400,088,381
US FEDERAL BUDGET DEFICIT $185,423,179,436
NET INTEREST ON DEBT $472,205,816,955
Revenues
US FEDERAL TAXES TOTAL $4,067,449,377,833
INCOME TAX $2,070,194,271,413
PAYROLL TAX $1,321,255,106,407
CORPORATE TAX $382,211,589,720
USDC US Debt Clock at Current Rates
US NATIONAL DEBT $22,668,432,266,520
DEBT PER CITIZEN $66,988
US FEDERAL SPENDING $4,392,210,062,089
US FEDERAL BUDGET DEFICIT $434,570,748,034
NET INTEREST ON DEBT $410,919,970,199
Revenues
US FEDERAL TAXES TOTAL $3,960,896,417,635
INCOME TAX $2,054,238,582,131
PAYROLL TAX $1,288,954,216,071
CORPORATE TAX $405,978,068,926

Taxes Throughout History

US Federal Marginal Top and Bottom Tax Rates 1913–2016

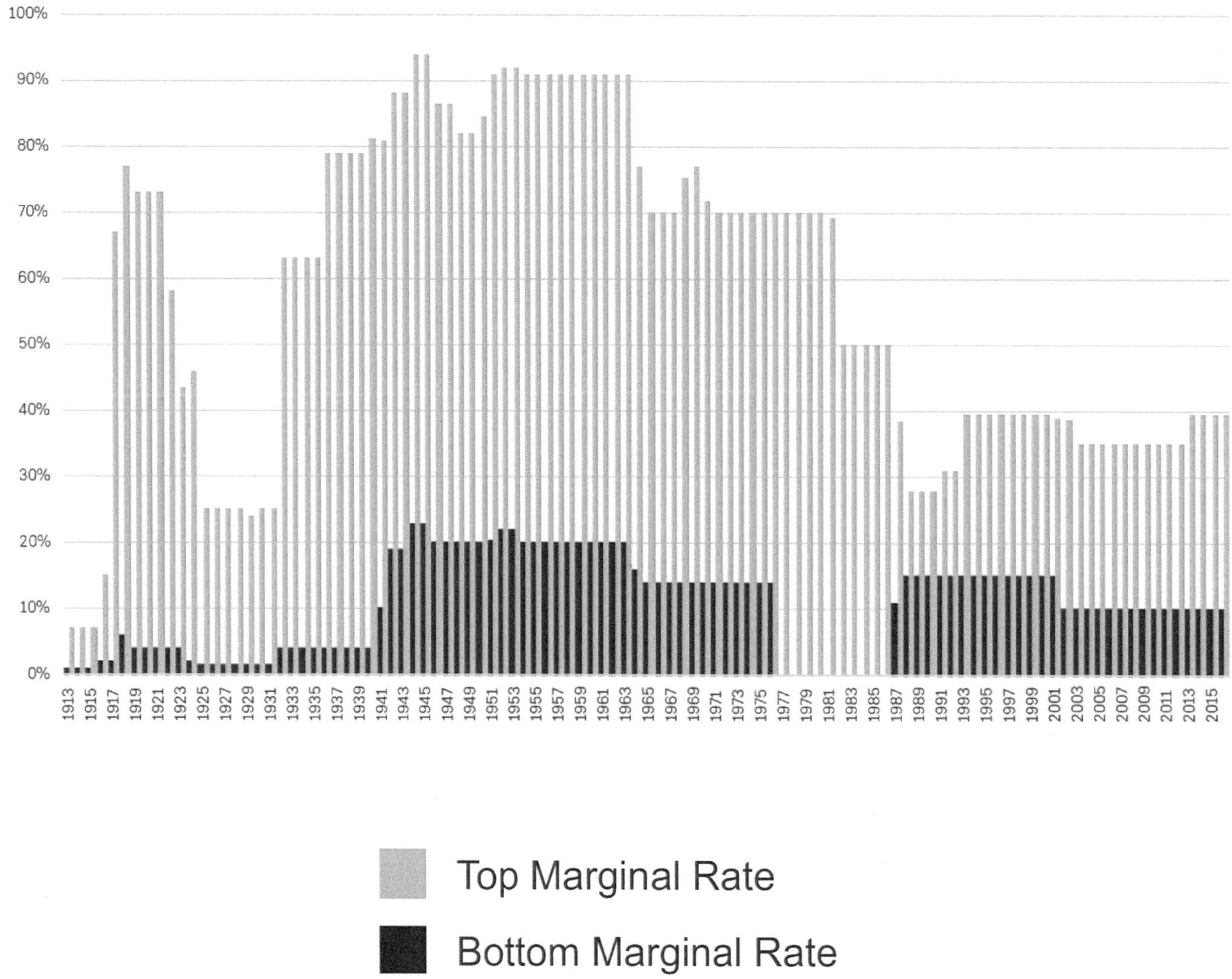

How Do Our Tax Rates Compare?

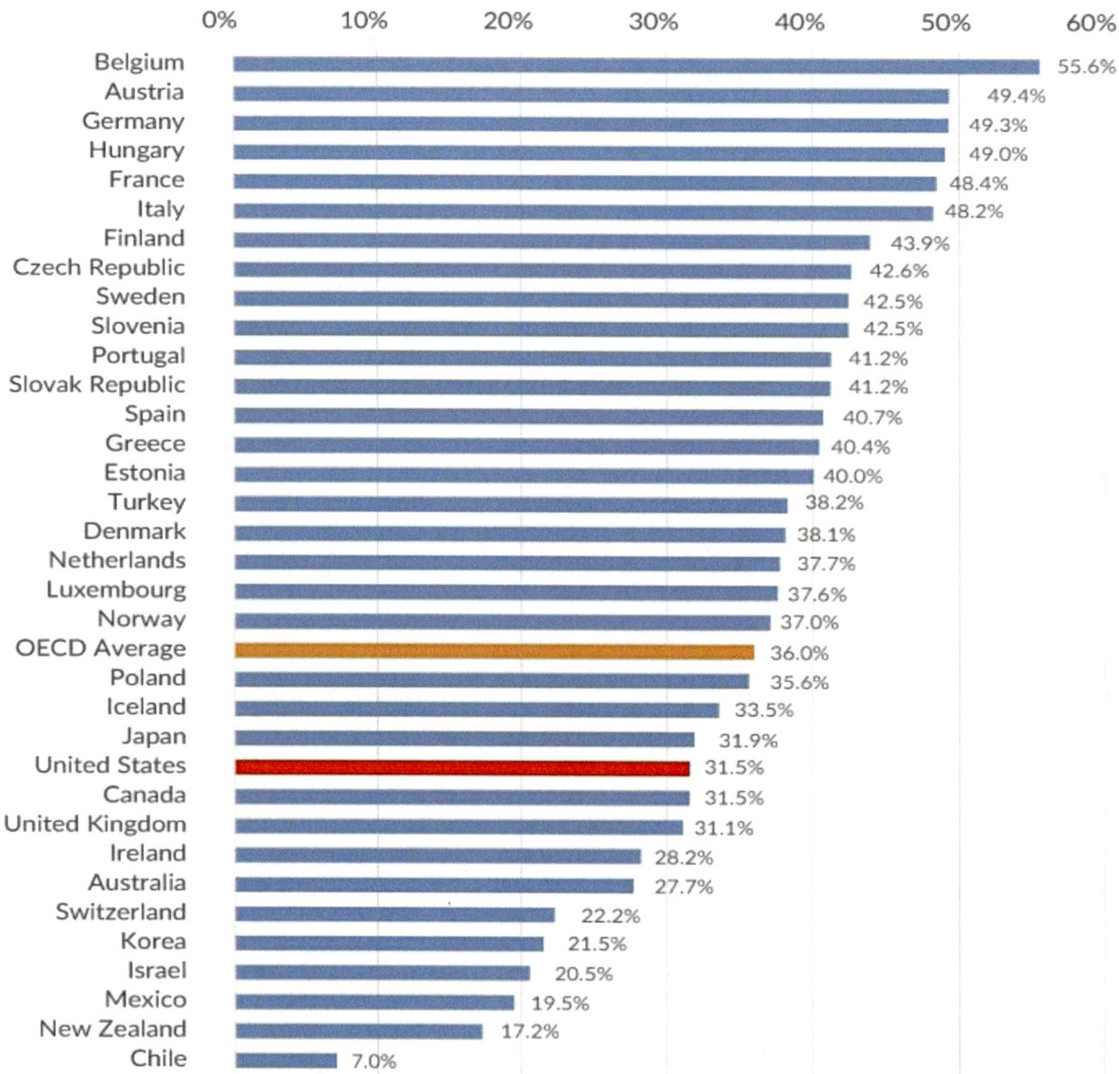

Source: OECD Taxing Wages, 2015.

Projected Cost of Interest on National Debt

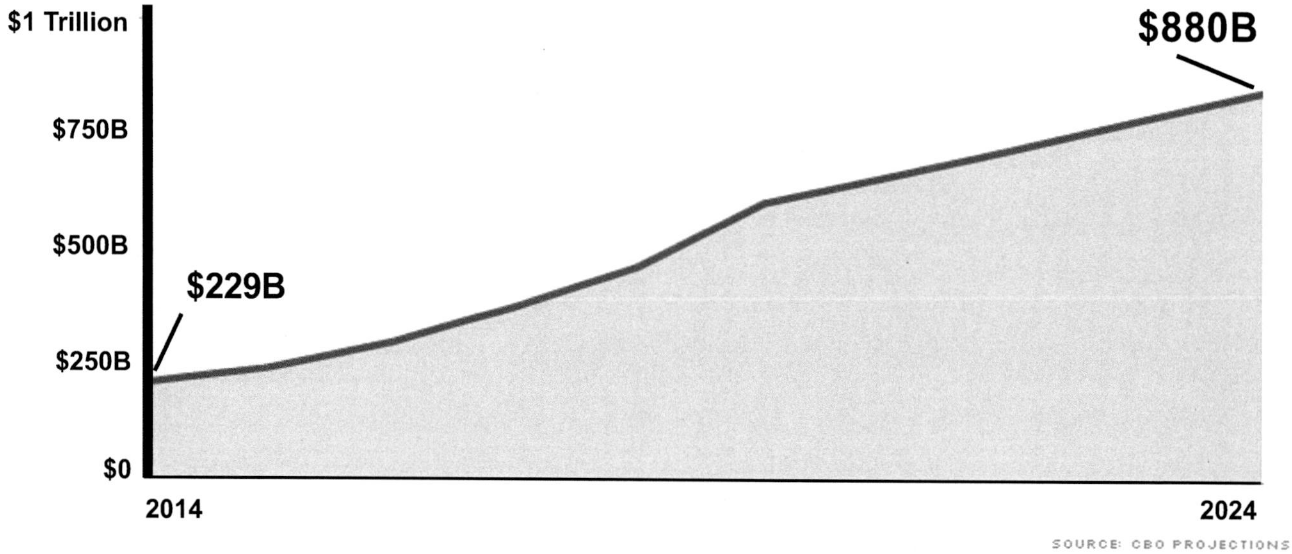

Source: https://www.cbo.gov/publication/45684

Steps to Take to Become More Tax Efficient

GET THE MATCH	• Take advantage of a **"match"** offered by your employer
ROTH CONTRIBUTIONS	• Make Roth contributions (no tax deductions, tax-free growth) • No income limit on Roth 401k contributions
ROTH CONVERSIONS	• Roth conversions on any tax-deferred accounts • No restrictions for age, income, wages, or amount allowed

A tax efficient plan that saves 5–10% is just like getting a 5–10% return.

Roth Conversion Example

Married Couple:

- Current Income: $85,000/year
- Taxable Income: $62,000
- Estimated Income in Retirement: $60,000/year

2001 Tax Brackets		
Rate	Single	Married Filing Jointly
15%	Up to $27,050	Up to $45,200
27.5%	$27,051-$65,550	$45,201-$109,250
30.5%	$65,551-$136,750	$109,251-$166,500
35.5%	$136,751-$297,350	$166,501-$297,350
39.5%	Over $297,351	Over $297,351

2018 Tax Brackets		
Rate	Single	Married Filing Jointly
10%	Up to $9,525	Up to $19,050
12%	$9,526-$38,700	$19,051-$77,400
22%	$38,701-$82,500	$77,401-$165,000
24%	$82,501-$157,500	$165,001-$315,000
32%	$157,501-$200,000	$315,001-$400,000
35%	$200,001-$500,000	$400,001-$600,000
37%	over $500,000	over $600,000

Efficient Income Streams

Section Objectives:

- The Value Proposition and Your Retirement Plan
- Efficient Income Streams

The Value Proposition

Return

- Proper asset allocation
- Is your **RETURN** greater than the **RISK** you are taking?

Risk

- Volatility (standard deviation)
- Average vs. Actual

Fees

- What are the total fees being paid?
- Are you getting what you paid for?

Taxes

- Growing your money in the "right account"
- Strategies to potentially pay lower taxes

Risk vs. Return

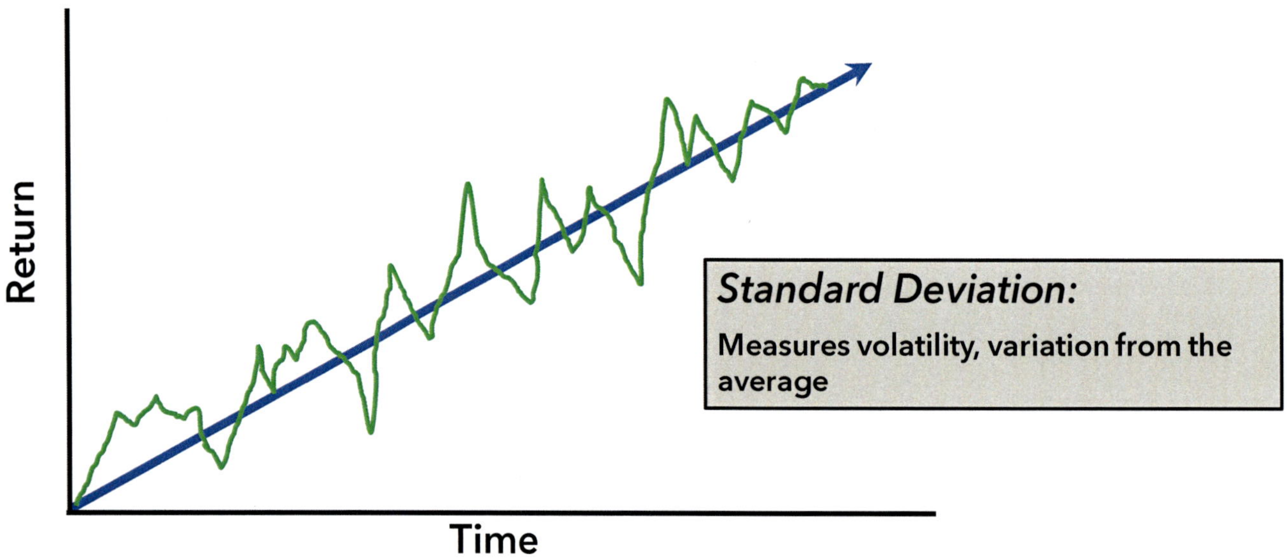

Rule of Thumb: The return should be higher than the Standard Deviation.

Risk vs. Return

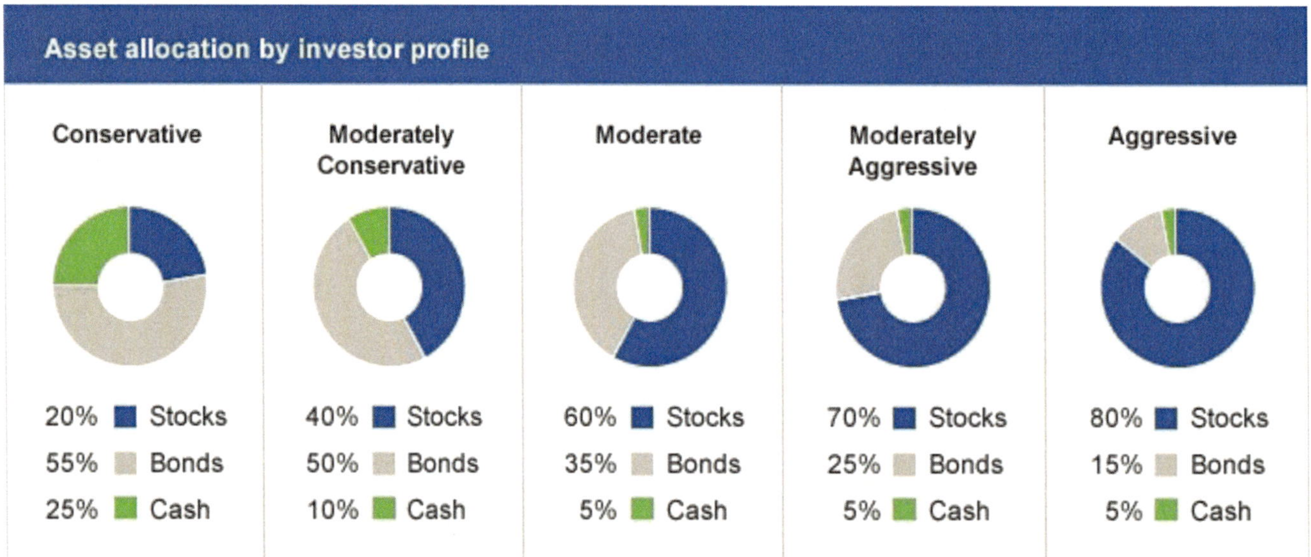

BUY & HOLD:
- **Usually lower cost**
- **High volatility**
- **Remains during correction**
- **Better potential returns if invested long-term**

TACTICAL:
- **Often more expensive**
- **Proactive action to help prevent losses** (lower volatility)
- **Better potential short-term returns**

Average vs. Actual Returns

KEY TAKEAWAY:

If you are getting VALUE:

- Tactical approach should generate more consistent returns

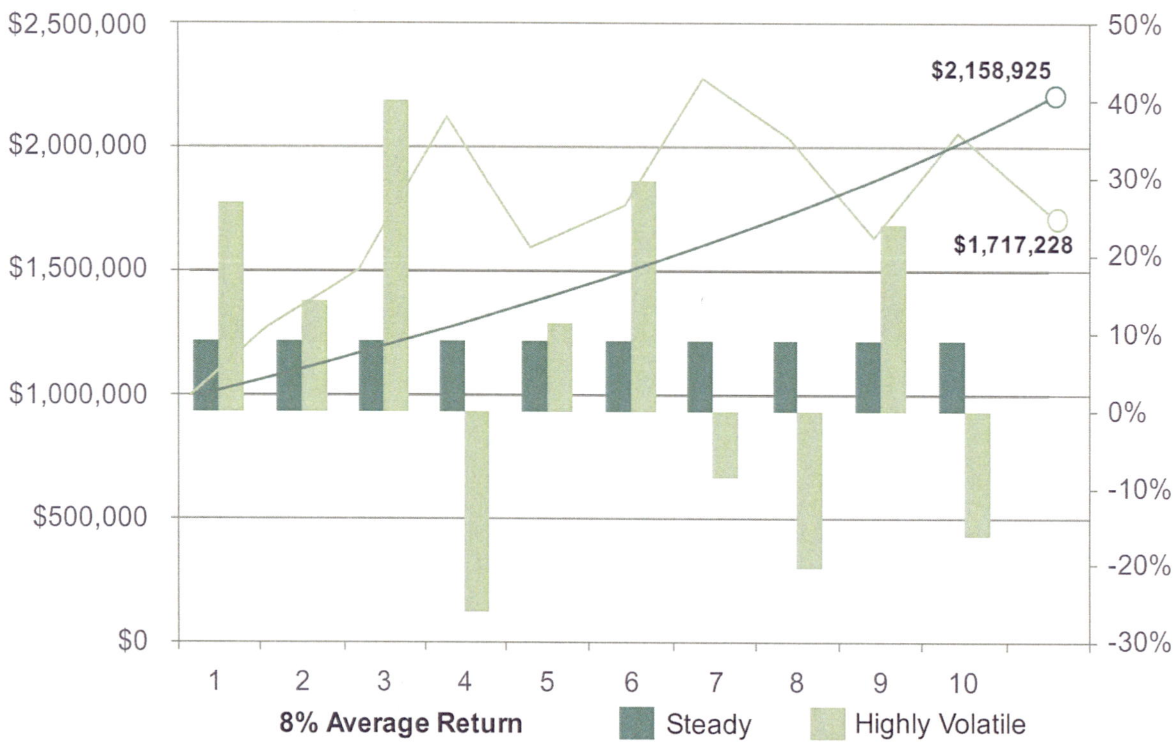

Note: The graph shown is hypothetical and does not represent any particular investment.

The Impact of Fees

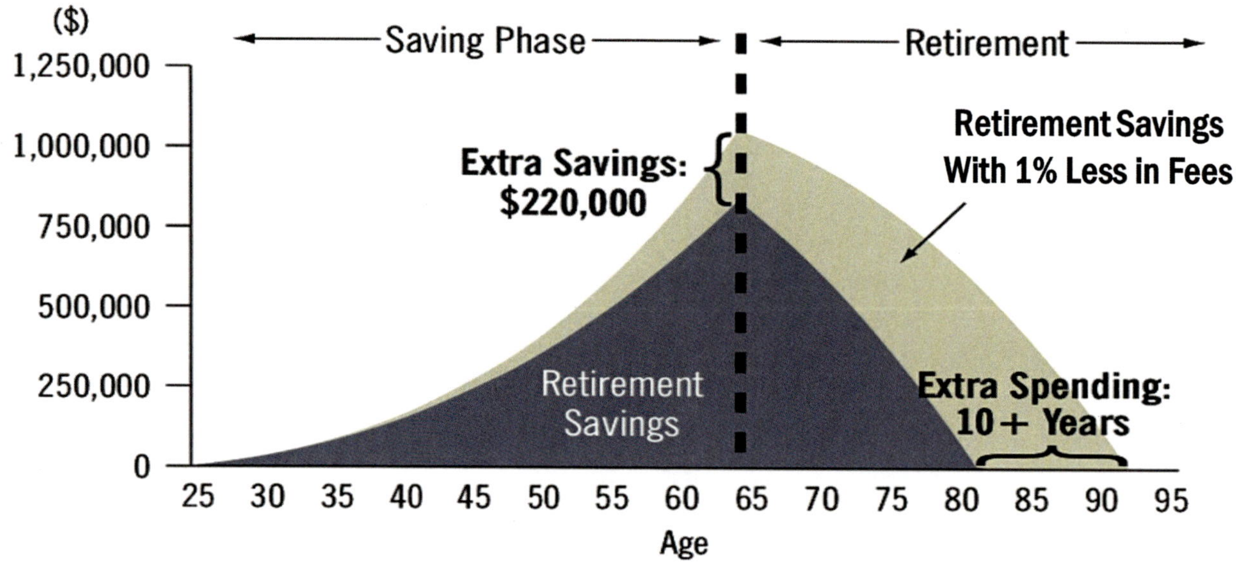

The saving phase simulates a salary of $45,000 increasing to $85,000, saving 8% per year increasing gradually to 15%. Retirement spending of $63,750 (75% of final salary). Rate of return of 9% assumed at age 25, linearly decreasing to 6% at age 80 and remaining constant thereafter. Source: AllianceBernstein

Tax Efficiency

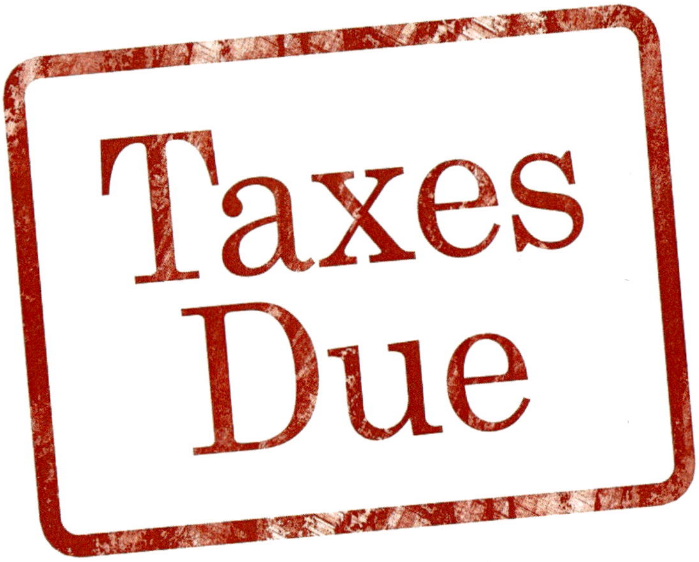

"You must pay taxes. But there's no law that says you gotta leave a tip."

- Morgan Stanley advertisement

KEY TAKEAWAY:
A tax efficient plan that saves 5–10% is just like getting a 5–10% return.

Efficient Income Streams

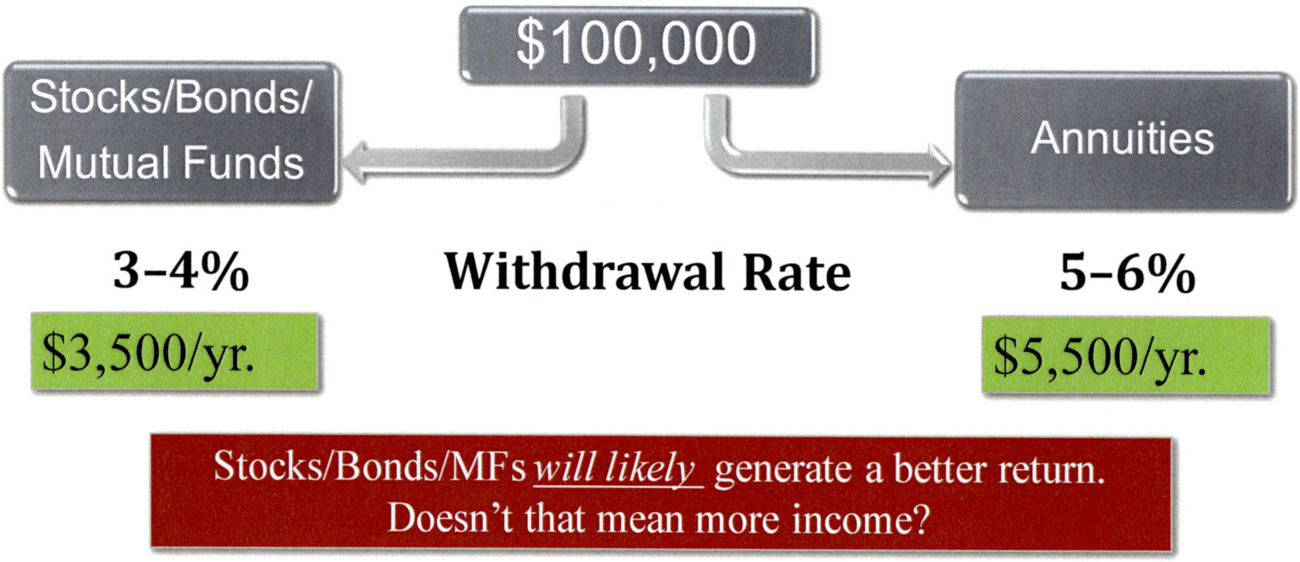

Efficient Income Streams

Option #1	Option #2	Option #3
Stock/Bonds/MFs	Fixed Indexed Annuity	Fixed Indexed Income Rider

	Option #1	Option #2	Option #3
Investment:	$100,000	$100,000	$100,000
Rate of Return:	**8.0%**	**5.0%**	**7.0%**
Balance after 10 yrs:	**$215,892**	**$162,889**	**$196,175**
Withdrawal Rate (Morningstar)	**3.5%**	**5.0%**	**5.0%**
Projected Annual Income:	**$7,556/yr**	**$8,144/yr**	**$9,836/yr**

Note: The illustration shown is hypothetical and does not represent any specific product.

Case Study

Section Objectives:

- How to apply the Keys to Success in the New Retirement

Case Study: Information into Action

Client Name: Jack Johnson **Age:** 63 **Social Security:** $2,000 (66)
Client Name: Sarah Johnson **Age:** 63 **Social Security:** $1,500 (66)

Investable Assets: **Qualified:** $790,000 **Non-Qualified:** $250,000

Client Notes:

- Client plans to retire in three years.
- They will need $75,000/yr. in retirement.
- Trying to decide when to claim SS benefits.
- Concerned about risk and not running out of money.

Social Security

- Claiming options

Tax Analysis

- Roth conversions
- IRA spend down

Portfolio Analysis

- Fee Analysis
- Risk & Reward
- Monte Carlo Simulation

Detailed Income Plan

- Income timing
- Income efficiency strategies

Case Study: Information into Action

Social Security

- **Claim at 67 or defer until age 70:**
  - If deferred, benefit would increase by 8% each year.
  - Benefits would increase from $3,500/mo. to $4,620/mo.
  - ***Would need to determine how to fund income needs from age 66–70.***

Tax Analysis

- **IRA Spend Down:**
  - If SS benefits are deferred until age 70, income would be at $0.
  - Money spent from the IRA would be withdrawn at the lowest tax brackets.
  - **Roth conversions:**
    - Analyze income each year to determine if funds can be moved to a Roth without going into a higher tax bracket.

Portfolio Analysis: Current Allocation

Portfolio Allocation

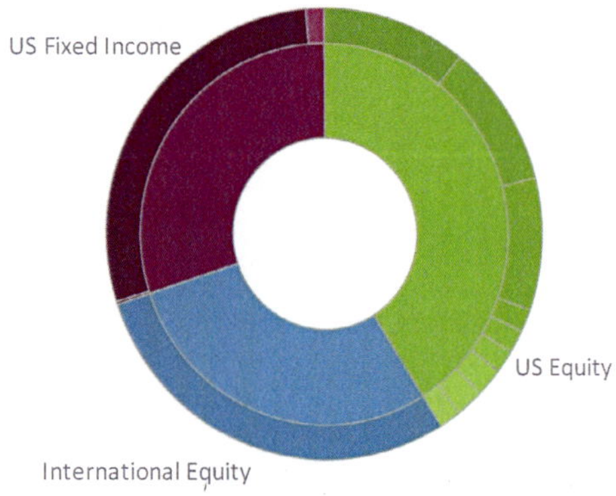

Risk vs. Reward Analysis

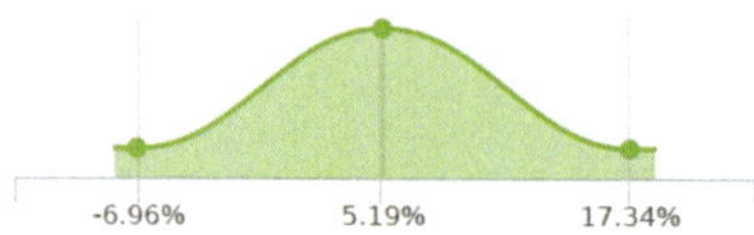

Annualized Return	Risk
5.19%	12.15%

**Risk is measured as the standard deviation of returns.*

**A higher standard deviation may result in greater fluctuation of the value of an investment.*

Monte Carlo Simulation

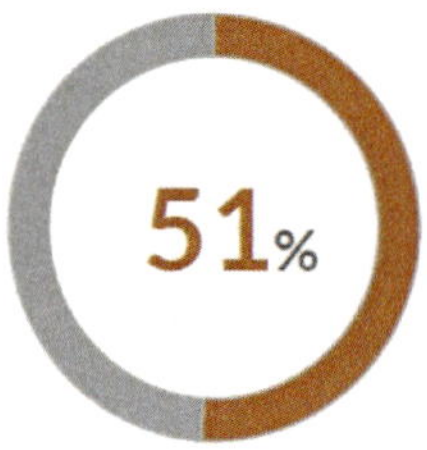

You have a 51% probability of attaining your outlined goals. This means that of the 1,000 simulations run, approximately 49% of the time you would exhaust your portfolio.

Actions to increase the probability of success may include increasing your savings, lowering your expenses, or adjusting your investment risk.

Portfolio Analysis: Tactical Allocation Only

Portfolio Allocation

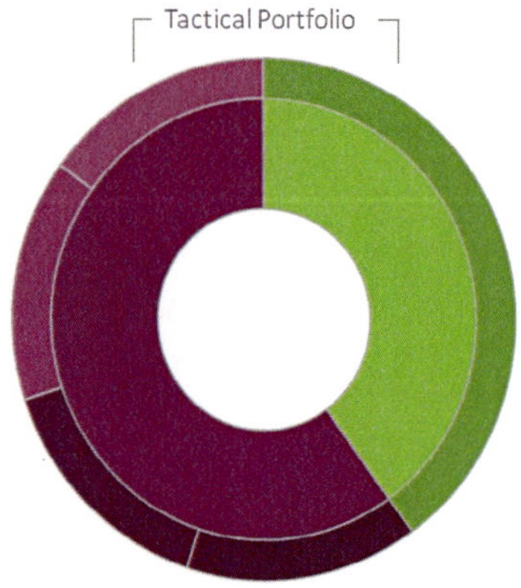

Risk vs. Reward Analysis

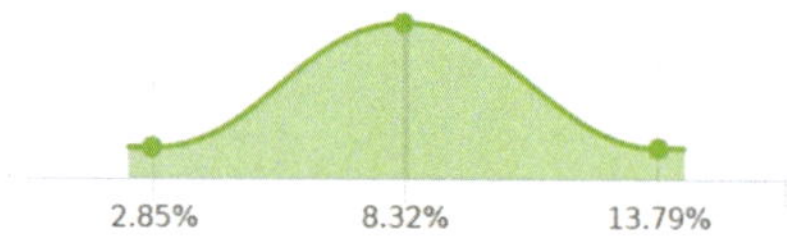

Annualized Return	Risk
8.32%	5.47%

**Risk is measured as the standard deviation of returns.*

**A higher standard deviation may result in greater fluctuation of the value of an investment.*

Monte Carlo Simulation

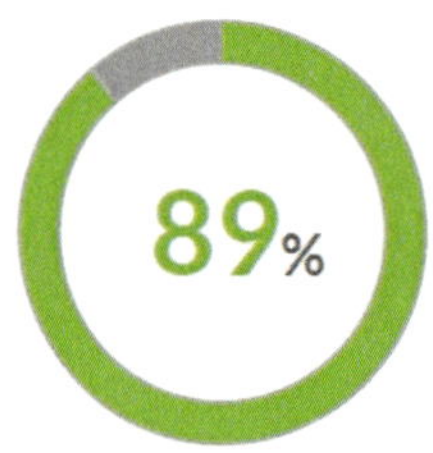

You have a 89% probability of attaining your outlined goals. This means that of the 1,000 simulations run, approximately 11% of the time you would exhaust your portfolio.

While the probability of success is acceptable additional steps to increase savings, lower expenses, or adjust investment risk could be implemented.

Case Study: Information into Action

Client Name: Jack Johnson **Age:** 63 **Social Security:** $2,000 (66)
Client Name: Sarah Johnson **Age:** 63 **Social Security:** $1,500 (66)

Investable Assets: **Qualified:** $790,000 **Non-Qualified:** $250,000

Client Notes:

- Client plans to retire in three years.
- They will need $75,000/yr. in retirement.
- Trying to decide when to claim SS benefits.
- Concerned about risk and not running out of money.

Social Security

- **Wait to claim until age 70**
  - $4,620/mo.
  - $55,440/yr.

Detailed Income Plan

- **Income shortfall:** Approximately $20,000/yr.
- **Income efficiency strategies:**
  - What is the most efficient way to provide the needed income?
  - How can we make sure they do not outlive their money?

Portfolio Analysis: Tactical Allocation & Annuity

Portfolio Allocation

Risk vs. Reward Analysis

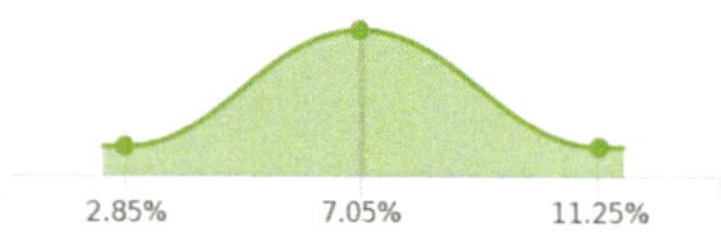

Annualized Return	Risk
7.05%	4.20%

**Risk is measured as the standard deviation of returns.*

**A higher standard deviation may result in greater fluctuation of the value of an investment.*

Monte Carlo Simulation

You have a 100% probability of attaining your outlined goals. This means that of the 1,000 simulations run, approximately 0% of the time you would exhaust your portfolio.

Detailed Income Plan

Year	Client/ Co-Client Ages	Beginning Portfolio Value	Total Net Income	Total Net Goals & Fees	Simulated Net Return	Ending Portfolio Value (Future Dollars)
2016	63/63	$1,040,000	$0	$0	1.40%	$1,054,595
2017	64/64	$1,054,595	$0	$0	19.50%	$1,287,888
2018	65/65	$1,287,888	$0	$0	8.33%	$1,421,056
2019	66/66	$1,421,056	$39,903	$81,955	5.29%	$1,448,086
2020	67/67	$1,448,086	$40,733	$84,413	4.50%	$1,463,364
2021	68/68	$1,463,364	$41,579	$86,946	10.36%	$1,560,042
2022	69/69	$1,560,042	$42,442	$89,554	5.87%	$1,596,609
2023	70/70	$1,596,609	$43,323	$92,241	2.82%	$1,585,995
2024	71/71	$1,585,995	$44,222	$95,008	4.70%	$1,591,285
2025	72/72	$1,591,285	$45,140	$97,858	-1.44%	$1,500,571
2026	73/73	$1,500,571	$46,077	$100,794	-5.50%	$1,351,239
2027	74/74	$1,351,239	$47,033	$103,818	16.58%	$1,490,901
2028	75/75	$1,490,901	$48,009	$106,932	5.68%	$1,494,747
2029	76/76	$1,494,747	$49,005	$110,140	6.07%	$1,500,953
2030	77/77	$1,500,953	$50,021	$113,444	8.25%	$1,535,076
2031	78/78	$1,535,076	$50,965	$116,848	13.43%	$1,643,112

Year	Client/ Co-Client Ages	Beginning Portfolio Value	Total Net Income	Total Net Goals & Fees	Simulated Net Return	Ending Portfolio Value (Future Dollars)
2032	79/79	$1,643,112	$51,730	$120,353	8.99%	$1,691,644
2033	80/80	$1,691,644	$52,505	$123,964	3.66%	$1,655,036
2034	81/81	$1,655,036	$53,293	$127,682	6.62%	$1,659,633
2035	82/82	$1,659,633	$54,092	$131,513	13.86%	$1,773,126
2036	83/83	$1,773,126	$54,904	$135,458	8.10%	$1,800,531
2037	84/84	$1,800,531	$55,727	$139,522	5.25%	$1,777,096
2038	85/85	$1,777,096	$56,563	$143,708	13.39%	$1,883,249
2039	86/86	$1,883,249	$57,412	$148,019	10.06%	$1,938,530
2040	87/87	$1,938,530	$58,273	$152,460	7.91%	$1,954,589
2041	88/88	$1,954,589	$59,147	$157,033	9.70%	$1,998,931
2042	89/89	$1,998,931	$60,034	$161,744	10.29%	$2,052,450
2043	90/90	$2,052,450	$60,935	$166,597	0.33%	$1,914,778
2044	91/91	$1,914,778	$63,032	$171,595	2.98%	$1,826,430
2045	92/92	$1,826,430	$64,047	$176,742	9.86%	$1,846,929
2046	93/93	$1,846,929	$70,064	$182,045	17.21%	$2,000,291
2047	94/94	$2,000,291	$71,161	$187,506	14.31%	$2,117,896
2048	95/95	$2,117,896	$72,276	$193,131	9.04%	$2,140,706

Case Study: Results

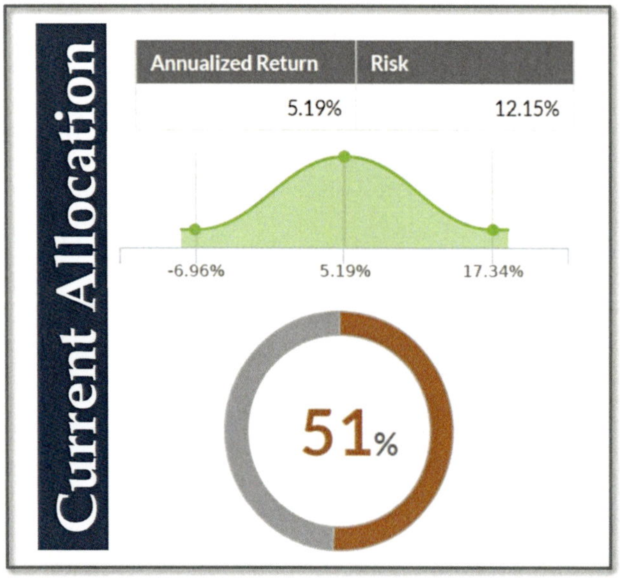

Success in the New Retirement

Do Your Homework
- Budget & Assets
- Social Security & Pension Benefits

Do Your Research
- Portfolio Analysis
- Value Proposition

Implement the Plan
- Reallocate investments
- Make adjustments as needed

> "It takes as much energy to wish as it does to plan."
>
> - Eleanor Roosevelt

> "Money is only a tool. It will take you wherever you wish, but it will not replace you as the driver."
>
> - Ayn Rand

Additional Notes

83345954R00097

Made in the USA
San Bernardino, CA
25 July 2018